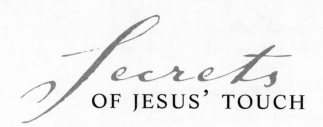

Secrets OF JESUS' TOUCH

TEN KEYS TO UNLOCKING THE POWER OF GOD IN YOUR RELATIONSHIPS

STEVEN MOSLEY

NAVPRESS®

Bringing Truth to Life

OUR GUARANTEE TO YOU

NavPress
P.O. Box 35001
Colorado Springs, Colorado 80935

The Navigators is an international Christian organization. Our mission is to reach, disciple, and equip people to know Christ and to make Him known through successive generations. We envision multitudes of diverse people in the United States and every other nation who have a passionate love for Christ, live a lifestyle of sharing Christ's love, and multiply spiritual laborers among those without Christ.

NavPress is the publishing ministry of The Navigators. NavPress publications help believers learn biblical truth and apply what they learn to their lives and ministries. Our mission is to stimulate spiritual formation among our readers.

ISBN 1-57683-402-6

Cover design by Ray Moore
Cover photo: Masterfile/Brian Pieters
Creative Team: Don Simpson, Amy Spencer, Pat Miller

Some of the anecdotal illustrations in this book are true to life and are included with the permission of the persons involved. All other illustrations are composites of real situations, and any resemblance to People living or dead is coincidental.

Unless otherwise identified, all Scripture quotations in this publication are taken from the HOLY BIBLE: NEW INTER-NATIONAL VERSION® (NIV®). Copyright © 1973, 1978, 1984 by International Bible Society. Used by permission of Zondervan Publishing House. All rights reserved. Other versions used include: the *New American Standard Bible* (NASB), © The Lockman Foundation 1960, 1962, 1963, 1968, 1971, 1972, 1973, 1975, 1977; and *The Message: New Testament with Psalms and Proverbs* (MSG) by Eugene H. Peterson, copyright © 1993, 1994, 1995, used by permission of NavPress Publishing Group.

Mosley, Steven R., 1952-
  Secrets of Jesus' touch : ten keys to unlocking the power of God in
your relationships / Steven Mosley.
     p. cm.
Includes bibliographical references.
  ISBN 1-57683-402-6
  1. Interpersonal relations--Religious aspects--Christianity. 2. Jesus
Christ--Example. I. Title.
  BV4597.52.M67 2003
  248.4--dc21
                            2002155430
Printed in the United States of America

1 2 3 4 5 6 7 8 9 10 / 07 06 05 04 03

FOR A FREE CATALOG OF
NAVPRESS BOOKS & BIBLE STUDIES,
CALL 1-800-366-7788 (USA)
OR 1-416-499-4615 (CANADA)

I am very grateful for invaluable input on the Secrets books from Phyllis Thomas, Shay Brown, and my own beloved Marilyn.

CONTENTS

INTRODUCTION

—— ⁂ ——

THERE ARE times when individuals electrify an entire population.

In 1956 Elvis was so hot he created a new phenomenon: the mass idol, sweeping America all the way from "Heartbreak Hotel" to "Hound Dog."

In 1965 The Beatles were so hot they pushed Shea Stadium, filled with 53,275 fans, into hours of hysteria.

In 1987 Michael Jackson was so hot he moonwalked all the way into pop deity, with "Bad" debuting at number one on the Billboard charts.

At certain moments in history, a star's charisma springs to epic proportions. He's the new thing, and everybody wants a piece of him. She embodies the times so powerfully, people start to invest their hopes and longings in her. They follow the star's every move in the tabloids. They imitate the star's every fashion quirk.

Amazingly enough, that's the way it was with an ex-carpenter from a sleepy Galilean town called Nazareth. If you really want to understand the Jesus phenomenon of the first century, only music stars in our time offer a parallel. Nothing in religion comes close.

We are used to seeing Jesus through various filters, of course. After all, he's a long way off, in terms of history. We have layers of theology that explain his teachings. We have church rituals that memorialize his actions. In other words, he's been institutionalized; we're removed some distance from the dazzling charisma of his person on this earth.

But seeing him live was something else. Jesus was mobbed wherever he went.

When he paused by the shore of Lake Galilee to give a discourse, such a large crowd pressed around him on the sand, he had to get into a boat to speak.

When he went to some "solitary place" on the other side of the lake, a huge crowd would be there waiting. People walked many miles from their villages just because word got out that he might be heading to a certain spot.

When they knew he'd be passing through a town, like Capernaum, the crowds that gathered "almost crushed him." Huge crowds "were trampling on one another" trying to get close.

When he stopped in at someone's house, the press of those wanting to get near this celebrity was so constant "he and his disciples were not even able to eat."

Jesus was what was happening. Jesus was the hot topic. The question flying around every village well, every marketplace, every sheep pasture was: Who is this Man from Nazareth?

Even when Jesus tried to keep the buzz down, asking men given their sight not to tell anyone, the news raced through Galilee: "People were overwhelmed with amazement. 'He has done everything well,' they said."

That was the understatement of people at a loss for words. Jesus raised healing and teaching and ministering to a whole new level. No one ever spoke like this man. No one ever cared like this man. And yes, no one ever touched like this man.

There were other teaching rabbis who dispensed wisdom to the crowds. There were others who claimed to heal. But he was The Master—"Nothing like this has ever been seen in Israel."

Jesus touched people in a way no one else ever had. And it was more than just a matter of removing illnesses or fixing twisted limbs. He was the Man with the Golden Touch. Almost everything and everyone he came in contact with was transformed. After his touch, individuals wanted to drop their lives immediately and take up a new one with him. That's charisma.

I believe the secret of Jesus' touch is beautifully expressed in one of his pictures of the kingdom: the laborer who uncovers a great treasure buried in an ordinary wheat field. Jesus had such a golden touch because he was constantly looking for hidden treasure. He saw every human being as a person with a great treasure somewhere inside. His touch uncovered it.

As we shall see, that's what Jesus did all over Judea and

Galilee. He left behind a trail of human beings staring wide-eyed at treasure dug up, sparkling in their hands.

In this book we're going to discover just how Jesus found hidden treasure. We're going to discover just how he touched people and what he touched in people that enabled him to have such an extraordinary impact during his three-year career. And that is going to show the way to great relationships, the way to empower the people around us.

The secrets behind Jesus' touch will reveal

How we can stretch, instead of just react.

How we can make great things out of the smallest of gifts.

How we can avoid turning boundaries into brick walls.

How we can learn the most from those who annoy us the most.

How we can inject hope into hopeless cases.

How we can stop quarreling for love.

How we can find faith in the unlikeliest of places.

Believers over the years have managed to preserve the principles on which Jesus Christ founded his kingdom. We've organized them into doctrines very well. But when it comes to charisma—that's another story. Today we're usually trying to defend ourselves and our children from "popular culture." Jesus *was* popular culture. Conservative religious groups are apt to be made fun of by sophisticates in "the world." Jesus aroused the envy of sophisticates in his world. We're always warning our young not to follow the crowd. Jesus couldn't go anywhere without attracting huge crowds.

We have the truth, but have we lost the touch—that sure touch, that surgically precise touch, that transforming touch? Our relationships can be empowered in extraordinary ways when we begin to understand this Man with the Golden Touch.

We've got the truth; we need to recover his touch.

Cited:

Crowd pressed around him—Matthew 13:2

A huge crowd is waiting—Luke 9:37

Almost crushed him—Luke 8:42

Trampling on one another—Luke 12:1

Not able to eat—Mark 3:20

Done everything well—Mark 7:37

Ever been seen in Israel—Matthew 9:33

THE NOISE OF INNOCENCE

BUSINESS COLLAPSED like an overburdened camel one afternoon in the courts of Jerusalem's gorgeous temple. The voices of those buying and selling hushed. They'd all been driven out by the big parade. Jesus had come to town, carried along in triumph by the fickle crowd that, today, was singing hosannas to the best man they'd ever known. The momentum of that parade, which had been building through Jerusalem's streets, overturned the tables of moneychangers and swept up the blind and the lame in its wake. Jesus' outstretched hand directed traffic and healed, both with equal force. Long-established merchants fled. An assortment of diseases fled.

As if that weren't enough of a disturbance, little kids began chanting a Jesus-the-Messiah cheer, loud as pagans egging a gladiator on at the Coliseum in Rome. Their shouts replaced the quieter, more orderly scams going on among temple moneychangers franchised by the priests. A different franchise had arrived, one whose first customers were the maimed and leprous, individuals who normally would never see the inside of the temple.

Chief priests and scribes, looking at this invasion of their

turf, played their roles predictably. Gathering up their indignation like an ancient scroll, they focused it, interestingly enough,
on the children. The formerly blind were babbling on about
color and shape. The formerly lame were jumping around like
acrobats. But the temple heavies wanted the kids shut up. "Do
you hear what these children are saying?" they asked in a huff,
sounding like a neighbor who yells at some neglectful parent:
"Are you totally unaware of the *noise* your kids are making?"

There was a good reason people like the Pharisees would
instinctively pick on the street urchins: Children represented
everything their religion did not. No two more opposite cultures
can be imagined.

Pharisee culture was about avoidance. Pharisees built elaborate precautions to avoid anything that might render them ritually unclean. Kids touch everything. Kids want to put everything
in their mouths; they smear everything on their faces.

Pharisee culture was about dissecting sacred texts and traditions. Kids swallow it whole.

Pharisee culture was about drawing lines that excluded.
Kids explore.

Pharisee culture was about rules that organize behavior
down to the details. Kids are forever bumping into the rules and
creating disorder.

So yes, of course the praises of those children sounded like
noise to the Pharisees. They could hardly stand those unstructured

noises bouncing off the massive stones of a temple where the smoke of offerings had ascended for thousands of years. The fact that the children were singing praises to their rival, Jesus, made it even more unbearable.

Stop the scene for a second and ask yourself a question: How did those kids get there in the first place? After all, they'd grown up in a culture dominated by priests and scribes of a certain persuasion, a culture that stressed the absolute submission of wives, children, and slaves. They knew they were supposed to be seen—at a distance—and not heard. How did they presume to lead out so boldly in the hosannas? How did they get so comfortable among the expert gatekeepers of the kingdom?

The answer is that these children had been touched. Something inside them had turned to gold.

One day a group of moms with toddlers joined the stream of curious and needy people approaching Jesus. They managed to nudge their way through the crowd and asked a couple of disciples if Jesus might lay his hands on their children. It was the custom to take your child at the age of one to be blessed by a rabbi.

Well, at that moment Jesus was busy explaining what the kingdom was all about. The adults were having a hard enough time grasping its principles; these kids couldn't even talk yet. So it was a bit annoying for the disciples to have to deal with yet another request for face time with the Master. They had to set priorities.

As the Twelve were ushering the mothers away, however, they heard Jesus stop his discourse and call out, "Let the little children come to me, and do not hinder them." The look on his face made the disciples get them to his side very quickly.

And then Jesus did something wonderful. He reached inside them, one by one, and found hidden treasure. He didn't just offer a pat on the head. He didn't just make condescending remarks about how strong a little boy was, how pretty a little girl was. No, he showed everyone that a great treasure waited to be discovered in these runny-nosed, restless kids on his knee. Looking around at his audience he said, "I tell you the truth, anyone who will not receive the kingdom of God like a little child will never enter it."

At that moment, the religious culture that enveloped Jesus did a giant "Come again?" There were white-bearded experts from synagogue who had devoted their entire lives to the study of how to get into the kingdom of God. And now Jesus was saying that the secret belonged to children—little squirts, no less! The ones who put everything in their mouths. The ones who were always touching the wrong thing. The ones who wouldn't know a guilt offering from a hole in the ground.

As these thoughts shot through the adults gathered around Jesus, he took the kids in his arms and laid his hands on them and blessed them. He was the Man with the Golden Touch that day. He'd given the children something no amount of ritual and regulation could stifle. It was something mothers and fathers would repeat as their toddlers started talking and understanding. It was something passed from kid to kid, a rumor on the playground about little children being first in line in God's kingdom—ahead even of Father Abraham.

That was Jesus' touch. He identified these children's irreplaceable role, their unmistakable value. Every day, every hour, they were showing their elders how to enter the kingdom of God. You just take it and stick it in your mouth. You just swallow it whole. You just show up. That's how you enter the kingdom— not as an expert, not after practicing for decades. You don't even enter it with a certain quota of faith. Kids are unaware they have faith. They just show up with whatever they have on hand.

Jesus had chosen the most unlikely candidates for admission as first citizens of the kingdom. That's why they showed up for the big parade. That's why they had the guts to walk right into the temple and shout the loudest praises on the day of Christ's triumphal entry. They belonged.

Jesus' spotlighting of children as the ones with keys to the kingdom is a great example of his golden touch. And it shows us something we all need to touch. There's a hidden treasure in our world waiting to be discovered. There's something in people that can turn to gold—with the right touch. And that's innocence. It's something we all too often overlook. It's something we're always rushing to get over, like a head cold. It's confused with ignorance or stupidity. People tend to mock it or apologize for it or spoil it.

But innocence actually has great potential. It's the fresh soil in which seeds sprout best. And it has its greatest potential when other people give it value. Innocence that's affirmed can grow into something more. We need to touch innocence. We need to touch it in a way that receives instead of just corrects.

How do we touch innocence? By embracing—instead of just reacting to—its noise. Innocence is often raucous and ragged. It doesn't slip seamlessly into the environment. Well, let it surround you. Let it sink in. Find the hidden treasure.

I've enjoyed swimming all my life, but I never knew what a delight water is until my three-year-old daughter jumped into a pool. I was holding her close as she splashed and squealed, and the look on her face went right through to me. I saw in the unedited excitement sparkling in her eyes all the pure joy God made us to experience.

It was only moments like this that enabled me to really grasp how preoccupied and numb and over-analytical I'd become. The wonder of a child's innocent pleasure is the perfect antidote for adult worry and stress. It's the doorway back into the kingdom of grace, where everything is a new creation.

In a secular age, we adults have our own counterpart to Pharisee legalism. Status and success and financial planning are how we get into the kingdom of the financially secure. We're experts in squandering life for money. We translate every meaningful encounter into a business opportunity. We're stuck on the Internet like a bug on a windshield, our quality time squashed on the screen.

Henri Nouwen had touched the best and the brightest as a professor of psychology and theology at Yale and Harvard. But he felt called to live in a community of the mentally and physically handicapped called Daybreak and there found his heart and soul deepened by touching "the least of these."

Innocence can come through someone who is a newborn in the life of faith. He's stumbling around, bumping into "church standards," not yet getting a handle on what he's supposed to do. His baby steps may be annoying. She may sing off-key, pray too loud, or jump to the wrong conclusions from stray verses of Scripture.

Well, we can cut him off; we can push him to the side; we can tell her to come back when she's got the routine down more smoothly. Or we can look for hidden treasure.

My faith never felt more alive than when I was trying to slip it between the bars of a county jail to a sandy-haired, wild-eyed young man who was hanging on for dear life. I was visiting with a group from my college. Josh was afraid his string of misdemeanors might land him in the state prison. He knew on some level that Jesus was his last, best chance of escaping the hellish life of abuse and violence and petty theft that was about to swallow him whole. He was trying to stay in the Word. Josh didn't know much. He might put Moses in the lion's den and Peter in the ark. But his raw struggle to affirm the basic truths of the gospel in a place where only the strongest survived left an unforgettable impression on me. I knew, in a way I did not before, the reality of the battle between good and evil.

How do we react to the innocence of the uninitiated? Do we have Jesus' touch? Or do we make them feel stupid because of all their questions? Do we see hidden treasure? *You've never read this story in John about the woman caught in adultery before?! Wow, tell me, what's it like, seeing it brand new? How does Jesus' intervention strike you?*

It's interesting to note just how Jesus responded to those huffing and puffing over the children's praises in the temple. He paused in his touching of the afflicted and asked them, "Have you never read, 'From the lips of children and infants you have ordained praise'?"

Innocence has a voice that glorifies God in ways the non-innocent cannot. The innocent see the world in ways others cannot.

Participants in the hundred-yard dash at the Special Olympics are racing wildly toward the finish line when one of them stumbles and falls to the track. The others glance back, then stop and come back for him. They pick him up and together jubilantly cross the finish line. We are forced to look at life in a completely new way.

Innocence isn't an absence of sight. It's eyes wide open.

Sometimes we try to create or preserve innocence by artificial means. We think that if we just shut our kids away from the world, their quantity of innocence won't diminish. It's certainly helpful to shield children from a barrage of sex and violence. But innocence isn't ignorance. It's not just sensory deprivation. It's a quality that takes in the world in a fresh, receptive way.

Innocence is a blank slate. Ignorance is an erased blackboard.

Innocence is the capacity to learn. Ignorance is lessons ignored.

Innocence is a sense of wonder. Ignorance is a dull stare.

Find hidden treasure in the noise of innocence. The mature, efficient, productive world tends to stifle those sounds. We're all in a library and the original noises of life have been sealed up in books, recorded in symbols. We don't experience anything for the first time anymore.

The innocent can show us how to enter the kingdom again.

I had a choice to make one afternoon as I sat admiring the nice cherry finish on my new executive desk. It was a big choice. Noises were coming through the closed double doors of my study in the house I'd just purchased. Three small boys were taking turns sliding down the stairs in a laundry basket, glee-fully screaming over every bump in the ride.

I was expecting a more peaceful setting as I began work on a television script. In fact, I had figured on a more peaceful set-ting that would last the rest of my life. Five years of being single, with my own kids off to college, had left me pretty attached to my comfortable routine. I did what I wanted when I wanted to. I had my quiet breakfast in a house heated to just the right tem-perature. I caught just the slice of news I wanted on *Today* while I shaved. I had just the right music playing when I started to write. No interruptions.

Now there was this racket. I had seen it coming, of course, when I married Marilyn. There had been noise before—the shouts of her kids in the park on a Sunday, for example, when I'd come to visit her. But this was different—day-by-day, hour-by-hour noise that besieges you in your own home while you attempt to earn a living.

So I had to decide what to do. Was I going to try to hang on to that uninterrupted life, that peaceful routine? Was I going to struggle to eliminate the noise and turn rambunctious boys into studious lads who played quietly and separately in their rooms every day? Of course I would sometimes have to tell them to be quiet. But how would I relate to the long noise of childhood in general? My instincts told me it was the enemy. I needed to build a wall around it.

But I tried something else. Grudgingly at first, I decided to embrace the noise of innocence. So, instead of just calling for quiet, I sometimes chased them around the house as Monster Steve. Instead of always insisting on tranquil, lazy evenings, I sometimes played hide-and-seek in the dark.

And what do you know: I discovered that my monster exercises actually helped me stay awake after lunch. More important, I found that having fun with the noise, instead of always fighting it, has kept me from many of the ruts of middle age. These boys rejuvenated me—in the nick of time, as fifty bore down on me and the recliner beckoned.

I have been blessed by the noise of innocence. It energized me in ways nothing else could have. So yes, I want to bless back.

The middle boy, Parker, is the more introspective one and developed a reputation for being whiny. He did seem to complain more than his brothers, and he felt it keenly when anything wasn't quite fair.

But after a few months of getting to know Parker (and several sessions of hide-and-seek), I noticed he hadn't whined much in a couple of weeks. So when one of his brothers made a crack about Parker the Grouch at breakfast, I said, "You know, I think Parker is really growing into Mr. Cheery. I don't hear him being grumpy at all. It's like he's this thankful, happy kid all of a sudden."

The comment passed; Parker just kept eating his Frosted Mini-Wheats, but it sank in deeper than I could have imagined.

After that, Parker became my best buddy. He wanted to get my advice on everything. He wanted to tell me about his day at school. But most remarkably, this boy hardly ever played the part of the Grouch again. He did grow into something else. I really realized it as Parker was presented a Student of the Month award at Circle View Elementary School and his teacher talked about what a courteous, helpful, all-around great kid he was.

The noise of innocence. It's a great place to look for hidden treasure. The right touch can turn it to gold.

Cited:

Temple visit—Matthew 21:10-16
Children blessed—Mark 10:13-16
Lips of children—Matthew 21:16

THE STARE OF A STRANGER

GENERATIONS OF mistrust loitered around the well like shadowy spies. Even the most common of gestures, like asking for a drink of water, could be taken as a provocation. The Samaritan woman and the Jewish traveler seemed to be stalking each other out there under a pitiless midday sun. The man was intent on exposing her innermost secrets. The woman didn't want to become easy prey.

Jesus had crossed a line at Jacob's Well. It was a line his culture had etched into him. Samaritans represented religious contamination. You didn't hang out with them. You certainly didn't take sustenance from them.

But Jesus just kept going further across the line. As he took in the cool drink this woman had finally been persuaded to winch up for him, he began advertising Living Water. He poked around in her private life—with the skill of a surgeon. He offered her everything she'd been desperately trying to obtain through five failed marriages.

And finally Jesus got through. Living water changed from a labor-saving device (Give me some of that water so I won't have to come out here every day to draw) into a spiritual reality ("Come, see a man who told me everything I ever did"). That water jar lowered into Jacob's Well eventually drew a whole village to the stirring knowledge that this thirsty stranger was the Savior of the world.

It was really an act of sabotage, Jesus' simple request of a Samaritan for a drink. It was something that exploded underneath the conventions that have always kept people apart, the prejudices that still keep Palestinians and Jews hurling suicide bombers and tanks at each other.

There was so much that should have kept Jesus on this side of the line that day: the woman's status as a gossip magnet; his reputation as a rabbi; the whole of Samaritan culture and its quirky theology.

But Jesus just wouldn't allow all these barriers to keep him from touching a human soul. And through a simple, courteous exchange, he made something as lofty as the indwelling Spirit as immediate and tangible as cool liquid on the tongue.

Jesus crossed clearly marked boundaries. That's part of the secret of his charismatic touch. He had a habit of interacting with the alien, the despised, the outwardly unattractive—and finding hidden treasure.

Nothing makes that clearer than his touching of lepers, the most unclean of all ritually unclean human beings in his culture. He didn't just send a polite word of blessing their way. He reached out his hand and touched their rotting flesh.

Jesus blurred the distinction between clean and unclean, much to the dismay of his spiritual elders. He disturbed their world built on elaborate precautions to keep people separate. Who's in; who's out? Jesus kept reversing the game. Unclean could become clean in a second. Health kept popping up where it had been banned. Hope kept springing up where it had been forbidden.

Jesus making contact at Jacob's Well, in fact, would grow into uncontainable treasure: the Gentiles flooding into the kingdom; the apostles preaching to every nation and tongue; the world turned upside down. This explosion of the church across all kinds of boundaries had its start that hot, stuffy day when Jesus reached out his hand to take water from a stranger.

And in that act Jesus shows us another way we can find hidden treasure today.

We live in a world where the boundaries have grown much more distinct, the walls much higher. Fanatics have upped the ante. Terrorists have knocked the ground out from under us. We thought holy wars were a relic of the Middle Ages. They're back with a vengeance. We thought bloodshed in the name of God a universal embarrassment. It's making headlines.

We're shocked at the hatred that drives people to randomly dispose of scores of men, women, and children. How do you protect yourself from individuals who don't mind blowing themselves up in order to make symbolic strikes against their enemy?

We don't have a good place to hide anymore. And of course we want to fight back. We feel like profiling a third of the planet. Maybe we should have a mandatory national ID card. Maybe we should speed through the trials of terrorists. Maybe we should lock the borders.

But the sad fact is, fear is how terrorism wins. Prejudice is how hatred wins. If mistrust starts to draw all the boundaries, we're going to live in a pretty cramped world.

We do need boundaries. That's especially true personally when it comes to toxic people. It's true as a nation when it comes to secure borders. But in times like these it's especially important to keep boundaries from turning into brick walls. We don't want to respond to people who terrorize by withdrawing into a shell. And it's here that Jesus' touch can liberate.

Jesus didn't reach across boundaries in Sunday school. He did it in a world of racial tension and Roman oppression. It was every bit as intense as a Palestinian refugee camp seething with frustration over the Israeli occupation.

Jesus dealt with his world of prejudice simply by touching one stranger at a time. It started at Jacob's Well. He didn't claim to understand Samaritan history and culture. He didn't claim to have a response to Samaritan grievances against his people. He just claimed to have an answer for one hurting woman.

The first step to making our world bigger is to stop claiming we know it all. I don't know what the Palestinian sense of occupation is like. I do not feel the passions that drive Protestants and Catholics to violence in Northern Ireland. I don't know about the mother's milk that ties a goatherder in Afghanistan to those dry hills. Accepting my own ignorance is the first step to transcending barriers. Nothing is more stifling to your soul than to assume you know the stranger. You don't.

That's why Laura Blumenfeld, the Jewish reporter who wrote *Revenge, a Story of Hope* (Simon & Schuster, 2002), got to know the family of the Palestinian who shot her father in the head. She fantasized about retribution. But she ended up peeling back her assumptions and eventually broke through her anger. She also broke through the prejudices of the Palestinian family to create an extraordinary bond.

Jesus' touch has never been more important—on a global scale, on a personal scale. He deliberately looked for hidden treasure in the stranger. That's his great antidote to fear.

Saul of Tarsus was one who believed in defending the faith by terror. He wanted to put the fear of his God into a troublesome sect hooked on the wrong Messiah. But he ran into something that turned his perspective inside out. There's a very good reason he changed from Saul the persecutor to Paul the nurturer. He adopted a very specific point of view in his life. This apostle wrote it down for the Corinthians: "For Christ's love compels us. . . . So from now on we regard no one from a worldly point of view." Because of Christ's reconciling love, Paul could regard no one in the old way, according to the flesh. He had to look at everyone through Christ's eyes.

What does that mean in practical terms? Paul told the Galatians what you *don't* do if you're looking through Christ's eyes: "There is neither Jew nor Greek, slave nor free, male nor female, for you are all one in Christ Jesus."

Christ's great act of reconciliation erases human distinctions. When it comes to racial and cultural and ideological boundaries, Jesus just doesn't get it. And *his* perspective is what matters. No dividing lines we draw can be significant after Christ shed his priceless blood for every human being on the planet.

What do you see in the stare of a stranger? Christ's love compels us to reach across barriers. We can perform our own acts of sabotage.

Choose conversation over fearful whispers.
Choose questions over assumptions.
Choose curiosity over suspicion.
Choose touching over pointing.

That's a space Jesus wants to occupy: "I was a stranger and you invited me in."

Who do you avoid? Who do you exclude? That's where you can find your next hidden treasure.

John began his gospel with a beautiful passage in which he described Jesus as the Word of God and the Light of the World. And he made this point: "The true light that gives light to every man was coming into the world."

Every human being, John asserted, has been touched in some way by the light of Christ. That's something we can honor. We can look past the barriers and try to find a reflection of that light of Christ glowing inside the stranger. That's the magic of Jesus' touch.

I realized how powerfully that perspective can impact individuals after our bus broke down in Tulsa, Oklahoma. We were fifty Illinois college kids trying to get home after EXPLO 72, Campus Crusade for Christ's big training conference in Dallas. We didn't know a soul in Tulsa. And we didn't think we wanted to. This was, after all, a world quite alien from our counterculture, Jesus-Movement, anti-establishment, hippie-friendly sphere. The Vietnam War was still hot to the touch. Tulsans, we assumed, were people who talked about what they'd like to do to flag burners while crooning, "I'm proud to be an Okie from Muskogee."

Most of the kids took a Greyhound north. Five of us stayed behind to try to get the bus fixed. We spent almost all our money; but the ancient yellow school bus still wouldn't run.

I remember it was dusk on a Sunday and the five of us huddled, standing on asphalt still hot from the summer sun. There didn't seem to be any way out of our predicament. Then we noticed people walking into a little stone Baptist church across the street for the evening service. We looked at each other. It was only desperation that drove us across the street.

As it turned out, the church folk were eager to help, especially a Mr. John Reed, who had a mechanic friend. "Why we'll have 'er runnin' in no time," he said cheerfully. "Ralph can fix most anything."

Ralph came over, but it soon became clear our ancient bus wouldn't be fixed that night. Mr. Reed—slightly balding, open-faced, and freckled—had an idea: "Listen, you all can come over and stay at our house." His wife, Evelyn, agreed: "We've got plenty of room. We'll get this thing going in the morning."

Gratefully, the five of us climbed into the Reeds' 1961 station wagon. We made our way to a modest home in a blue-collar neighborhood. A couple of sleeping bags on sofas here, some cots on the screened porch there, and everyone was settled.

It took a good part of the next day to find engine parts. John drove us around, pointing out the "sights." Other men from the church came in the evening. They joked together, drank Evelyn's coffee, and installed the parts, while we college types stood around pretending to assist. Finally, our bus started in earnest. The men cheered, had a final cup, and departed into the night.

Tuesday morning, after a savory meal of biscuits, scrambled eggs, bacon, and grits, we boarded our purring vehicle and thanked the Reeds profusely. We had nothing but thanks; they had provided everything else. Chris, the lone girl in our group, shed a few tears as we waved from the windows and pulled out.

We'd only gone a couple of blocks through the suburbs when our bus suddenly started screeching. My buddy Ron and I jumped out and opened the hood. We stared at the engine for what seemed a respectfully long enough time, slammed the hood down, and jumped back in.

Pulling up noisily at the now-familiar, blue frame house, we smiled sheepishly at John Reed and explained, "It started making awful noises."

This time it took two days to fix. But the Reeds remained gracious: "Great, you kids can come to prayer meeting with us."

On Wednesday evening we joined them at the little Baptist chapel. A warbling organ cranked out hymns that I had always thought rather dull. But that night, singing among those square jaws and weathered faces, I caught a new warmth from the old familiar phrases.

Pastor Johnson asked if we would get up and "testify" about the Lord's blessing at our conference. One by one, the five of us went up to the creaky wooden platform and talked about what we'd learned. John and Evelyn, looking like proud parents at a graduation, beamed at us as we mumbled our words of witness.

Thursday morning brought another tearful farewell. Our bus lumbered along amiably for an entire mile before falling fast asleep in third gear. It couldn't be coaxed awake before a highway patrolman dropped by. He insisted the vehicle be towed off the narrow road immediately, across town to Ace Garage.

I cringed as I dialed John's number. "Mr. Reed, it's me again."

"Well, I'll be. How far did you all get this time?" John wasn't upset. His voice sounded as affable as ever. "You sit tight, hear? We'll be over in a jiffy."

That day the five of us feasted on fried chicken, green beans, and corn on the cob. In the afternoon Chris looked at old photo albums with Evelyn, and the rest of us touched up the front siding. It felt good to be just family.

Friday morning. "This is going to be it," we said confidently, downing our eggs, bacon, and grits. We waved to "Mom" and "Papa" Reed again through the bus windows and they stood for a long time on their cramped crabgrass lawn.

At the outskirts of Tulsa, our crotchety yellow vehicle started hinting. Little groans here and there: *all is not well*. The motor misfired; the hinting grew more persistent. Ron and I grimaced at each other and finally decided to turn around; there was no way we'd make it back to Illinois.

What would the Reeds say this time? Surely they wouldn't believe it; surely we'd catch a hint of tension in their faces. But no, Papa was out on the lawn, waving us home as soon as our telltale sputtering could be heard coming up his street. We apologized lamely, but John wouldn't hear of it: "Glad to have you back."

During our entire stay in Tulsa we never saw a trace of the

wearying strain that must come from having five extra people camp out in your home. The Reeds always managed to make us feel like we were honoring them, not they us.

One guy in our group was black. The neighbors could not quite conceal their distress that someone like him was sleeping in their midst. But John told me quietly he was proud to be sheltering the young man.

We had popped uninvited out of a war-protesting, drug-and-sex-infested university environment into their Okie land of country music and the flag. We had absolutely nothing in common except Jesus. But that was enough. Mom and Papa Reed always treated us as a blessing—extra toothbrushes, sleeping bags, dirty socks, and all. They simply assumed we had some hidden treasure inside.

Saturday arrived, our fourth attempt at departure. We embraced our adopted family and said hopeful, sad good-byes. This time Chris's tears were not shed in vain.

The following Christmas my family took a trip south to visit relatives in Texas. We were passing by Tulsa on a Sunday when I suddenly remembered the chapel close by the freeway and talked my parents into stopping for a few minutes.

When I stepped inside the chapel, the worship service was almost over. During the closing hymn I exchanged excited glances with the Reeds.

We met outside under a high noon sun, and their joy bowled me over. Before then, I don't think I really knew what it meant to be "greeted in Christ." Papa Reed kept telling my dumbfounded parents what a tremendous boon we students had been to their church.

Those people's inexplicable delight just because I was present struck at something marrow-deep in me. John's youngest, a seven-year-old girl, had been away at summer camp during the broken-down-bus episode. The child had never laid eyes on me, but she rushed over anyway, across the boundary to a stranger, and hugged my waist earnestly, as if I were a long-lost brother.

At that moment I felt I was poured into being. It hadn't been that long since I'd crawled out of adolescence. Deep inside I was still a little kid trying to impress my peers, trying hard to acquire the with-it clothes, the hip tastes, the right personality. But that little girl's touch swept aside all those things. I had nothing with which to recommend myself. I became empty, illuminatingly so, and in that sudden vacuum experienced the grace of being poured full by their jubilation.

It is something I carry with me to this day.

Cited:

Jesus at Jacob's Well—John 4

Christ's love compels—2 Corinthians 5:14,16

Neither Jew nor Greek—Galatians 3:28

I was a stranger—Matthew 25:35

Light to every man—John 1:9

THE SMALLEST GIFT

HAVE YOU ever seen a movie so good you didn't want it to end? Have you ever been so visually and emotionally captivated you almost didn't want the plot resolved? Something like that was happening on a green hillside one afternoon by the Sea of Galilee. It wasn't Edwards Cinemas at the mall. It wasn't tens of millions of dollars in special effects. It was just one man speaking about life. But the crowd hung on his every word. They listened past distraction, past lunch, past supper.

That's when the disciples started getting nervous. Over fifteen thousand people were sitting there with nothing to eat, and it was a long walk home. They needed to go get food and lodging in nearby villages before everything closed down.

Jesus, however, uttered one of his perfectly ridiculous commands: "You give them something to eat!"

They stared at each other, as they'd stared at each other many times before. What could the Master be up to? Philip noted it would take a year's wages to feed the crowd. Judas clutched the moneybag tightly. Andrew found a kid who wanted to share his lunch.

But it was such a small gift—five barley loaves and two fish. Still, seeing so many mouths to feed, Jesus took it and gave thanks. Then the miracle happened. He put his hands on the bread and fish, and they multiplied like a single broken body providing nourishment for a whole world.

The entire crowd ate their fill. The leftovers alone—twelve baskets full—dwarfed the original gift.

It was through this sign, laid out above the shimmering blue lake, that Jesus began to illustrate his New Economy of the kingdom. The old religious economy was based on scarcity. Holiness was hard to get and acceptance hard to come by, so you saved every scrap you could scratch up. You accumulated as much as you could with the right rituals and ceremonies.

Jesus proposed an economy based on abundance. His perfect life accumulates more than enough merit for everyone. After telling a crowd about the lilies that are clothed and the sparrows that are fed, Jesus said, "Do not be afraid, little flock, for your Father has been pleased to give you the kingdom." Worthiness and acceptance are the starting points.

In the New Economy, small gestures become the whole. Abraham's act of looking up at the stars and believing God's promise is counted as righteousness—all of it. Abundance, not scarcity, is the rule. So a gesture of faith gets us into the bank vault of holiness.

Little things produce huge results. The slightest touch of the hem of his garment, in the midst of a jostling crowd, reverses twelve years of bleeding. The simplest of suggestions—throw your nets on the other side of the boat—brings in a record-breaking catch. A couple of stern words calm a storm.

Little things can hide great treasure. Unfortunately, human nature usually bends us in another direction: The bad little stuff annoys us to death. The good little stuff slips right by.

It happens every day. The insensitive remark we overheard by the water cooler rains on us all afternoon. The compliment the boss grudgingly tossed out dissolves into thin air. The acquaintance who laughs way too loud grates on our nerves; the gracious bit of self-effacing humor behind it doesn't register.

Missing a promotion can depress us for months. Getting one gives us joy for only a couple of days.

The bad stuff wears clodhoppers. The good stuff walks around on stocking feet. That's our human condition.

Jesus' touch with the bread and fish, however, tells us there are gifts out there, hidden in little things. There's buried treasure. It doesn't come nicely labeled and wrapped in a box. We're likely to need to brush off a little dirt and take a closer look.

Simply put, the New Economy of Christ's kingdom asks us to see more gifts than take-aways. The usual assortment of perils and hurts in life can predispose us to perceive only take-aways. Someone or something is trying to take stuff from us—take away our time, take away our money, take away our security, take away our status. When we're looking for take-aways, we find them. We clutch the stuff we've got more tightly. We clamp down on relationships. We hoard the upper hand.

We end up living in scarcity instead of abundance.

Jesus' generous touch suggests we look for gifts. When I wake up I can know God is up to something good. As I get dressed I can know gifts are multiplying out there. Today I can pick up wise whispers amid the racket, pageantry in the clouds, good news tucked away in some forgotten envelope. I can catch random acts of good will before they hit the ground. I don't look a gift source in the mouth; I just accept it.

Paul tells us, "God chose the weak things of the world to shame the strong. He chose the lowly things of this world and the despised things—and the things that are not—to nullify the things that are." That's part of Christ's economy of abundance. Why frantically hoard resources if the Father can do so much with so little? He turns the despised and the lowly into great treasure. He creates a new nobility of the small.

Just spotting little gifts, however, is not enough. We also have to use them. We have to take the barley loaves and break them. That's part of Jesus' touch.

As a producer, I get quite attached to a shooting schedule, and equipment or crew failures easily bend me out of shape. It was that way even back in college when I first started to do films. One afternoon, several rolls I was expecting to edit didn't come back from the lab. I'd made meticulous plans. My whole day was ruined.

But God had been trying to nudge me out of this rut in several ways. I'd begun to realize I should look for a gift in the empty space. So I took a deep breath and asked God to show me what I might do with it.

Wandering around the dorm, I ran into Shawn, a freshman still trying to fit in. He was going to pick up a package from home. I decided to go along, as if I had nothing better to do, and he was happy for the company.

As a result, I got to know Shawn quite well. He joined a Bible study in my room. And slowly he revealed some wrenching problems. A father who'd disowned him. A sexual addiction he agonized about. This was a kid who'd even contemplated suicide.

I was blown away. A few weeks before, I'd heard there'd actually been suicide attempts at the nice Christian campus where we were sheltered. It made me think I was pretty clueless about other people's problems. People right next door. And so I'd asked God to lead me to one. At least I could be friendly.

And there he was, sitting with some of my buddies on the floor of our dorm room, reading about Jesus and the paralytic. I managed to stick by Shawn that final year in college, through all his dramatic ups and downs.

It would have been so easy for me just to rant and rave about the stupid lab that screwed up my schedule. And all too often I did just that. But for once, God got through with the possibility of a gift I could uncover. He created a significant rendezvous out of an empty afternoon.

Jesus' touch inspires us to believe that the smallest of gifts can make a big difference. They can turn to gold. Psychologists are just beginning to document how important this is. Today more and more researchers are zeroing in on the "protective factors" that enable children to survive abusive homes and adults to bounce back from trauma. Dr. Albert Bandura, a pioneer in the field from Stanford University, identified the key ingredient in resilience, in the ability to overcome stiff odds. He calls it "self-efficacy," the belief that action will produce results.

That may not sound very startling. Doesn't everyone believe that actions will produce results? The answer is no. Victims don't. People who are overwhelmed by adversity don't. Some individuals come to believe that what they do won't really make a difference. They feel helpless. They just go with the flow. They remain captive to their urges. And what they don't realize is that it's these very assumptions that keep them trapped in a bad environment.

Self-efficacy is the conviction that I can change things. It's the assumption that I am responsible for my life. And that's exactly what Christ's charismatic touch inspired.

He wanted the paralytic to try to get up and walk. Just make the attempt. That gesture of faith can make something wonderful happen. In an environment where everyone had given up, where they were just waiting for a cure like people waiting to win the lottery, Jesus stepped in and said, "Rise, take up your mat."

He wanted the hemorrhaging woman to reach out to him through the crowd.

He wanted the fish-less disciples to go ahead and throw the net out again—on the other side of the boat.

He wanted Zaccheus to take a chance and invite him to dinner.

He wanted Martha to just stop and sit and listen.

He wanted people to roll away the stone from Lazarus's tomb.

These were small actions in the face of overwhelming disease and spiritual decay and even death. But they were aimed in God's direction. That's what produces the greatest results. What you do in God's direction is amplified. You start out with "What are these barley loaves among so many people?" You end up with "I can do all things through Christ who strengthens me."

One day Jesus spotted a widow sidling up to the temple treasury to drop in a couple of copper coins. All around her, wealthy donors were pouring in bagfuls of gold pieces. Jesus told his disciples she'd put in more than all the others combined. Well, no amount of creative accounting could make those two figures balance.

But in the New Economy, they did. In a world of abundance

they do. That widow's offering has multiplied in generous giving down through the centuries.

This is the difference Jesus' golden touch makes. The foolish and weak trump the proud and strong. That's a promise. When we give it all, the widow's mite really does become a fortune; ordinary water does turn into wine.

No one in Bruce Olson's high school would have ever picked him to become a hero among the fiercest tribe of the Colombian Amazon.* No one in their right mind.

Bruce was the kid everyone else didn't want to be. Spindly and pale, nearsighted and awkward, he lived in his own world of books and actually enjoyed reading Latin and Greek. While all the other kids were listening to the Beach Boys and the Rolling Stones, he was practicing dead languages.

Most painful of all, Bruce felt like a stranger in his own home. Someone was always fighting. His dad remained a distant, critical figure.

But then one day Bruce discovered hugs. They came by the score at a community church his buddy Kent invited him to. Surrounded by warm, friendly faces there, Bruce was persuaded

---

*This story is recorded by Bruce Olson in *Bruchko* (Altamonte Springs, Fla.: Creation House, 1992).

that Christ actually liked him. After making a commitment to this Savior, he began to feel alive for the first time in his fourteen years: "I didn't ever want that peace, that stillness to go away."

Unfortunately, when he tried to share this with his peers, they turned away and gave each other looks. When he tried to share this with his parents, they shut him out even more. Bruce wasn't very good at sharing his faith. He wasn't very good at anything.

But the affirmation at Kent's church continued. And it began getting to him. He absorbed something at this place where Jesus' touch was celebrated. It happened after a mission conference in which guest speakers talked about the amazing things God was doing among "unreached peoples." One morning Bruce woke up and felt a little gift growing inside him. Considering his background, it was the last thing he expected: compassion. Bruce felt a pang of compassion for the people of the various cultures the missionaries had talked about.

The little gift didn't go away. It stayed with him as he began studies at Penn State to become a linguist. And finally, after he turned nineteen, he decided to make the most of it. The kid got on a plane and headed to Caracas, Venezuela.

Bruce grabbed a little language and medical training and then, against everyone's advice, headed off into the rainforest of Colombia. Bruce had no business being there, of course. He had no background in missions or theology. He had no experience with cross-cultural communication. He had no sponsoring organization. He was a strange kid in the middle of a jungle who wouldn't last two days on his own. Back home, when his mom dropped him off for Boy Scouts he'd always sneak away to a drugstore and buy a book to read.

Bruce had absolutely nothing going for him except a little gift burning inside: he felt connected somehow to stone-age tribes of the Amazon. And he believed that could make a difference.

Soon Bruce stumbled on the Motilones. They'd killed just about every outsider who had set foot in their territory, and they almost killed Bruce. Incredibly, he survived the ordeal and managed to win their trust.

What happened next has been described as the most extraordinary example of positive development among an indigenous people group. In a few short years Bruce had established eight health stations, each one staffed by Motilones who gave shots, antibiotics, and other medications. This enabled the tribe to combat the epidemics that were wiping them out.

Each Motilone village also developed its own agricultural system. By raising corn and cattle they were able to have a much more stable diet.

And most amazing of all, the gospel had swept through the Motilone world like a brush fire. It didn't come just through Bruce's preaching. It came as a revelation, as a fulfillment of the hopes and prophecies of their own tribal folklore. The Motilones had been plagued by a peculiar indifference to the suffering of others that kept them from working together well. Colombian settlers were taking advantage of them and encroaching on their land. But now, united around Jesus, whom they'd awaited for countless generations, the Motilones became a strong, cohesive group.

Bruce Olson's exploits have won him the friendship of five presidents of Colombia and appearances before the United Nations and the Organization of American States. His was just a little gift that loving believers touched awake. It all happened because this kid, who felt utterly ungifted otherwise, felt a pang of compassion, a sense of connection. You can see it in the way he helped the Motilones deal with an outbreak of pinkeye that was threatening the tribe.

Pinkeye is easily treated with antibiotics. But the Motilones wanted no part of Bruce's medicines. That was for white people. Instead they kept going to their folk healer, who spoke long incantations over their sore eyes.

Bruce didn't want to destroy their traditions. So he made a decision. Approaching a man who had a particularly bad case of pinkeye, he rubbed his own finger in the corner of the man's eye. Then he smeared the pus in his own eye.

Soon he had a serious infection. But he didn't just apply an antibiotic on his own. He went to the Motilone healer for help. First he allowed her to sing her incantations. These didn't help him any more than anyone else. Then he went to her again and handed her some Terramycin. He asked her to apply that to his eyes as she sang her songs.

In three days Bruce's eyes had cleared up and he felt fine. After that he persuaded the woman to apply the antibiotic to others, and soon the whole tribe was cured.

That's Jesus' touch.

Somebody valued a gift and it grew. It produced transformation where there should have been disaster. It created a hero out of a reject. It was the smallest of gifts. But it turned to gold.

Cited:

Multiplying bread and fish—Mark 6:35-44; John 6:4-13

Pleased to give you . . .—Luke 12:32

Weak things shame strong—1 Corinthians 1:27-28

THE MESSINESS OF AFFECTION

JESUS AND his disciples had been invited to a festive supper six days before Passover in the home of Simon, a Pharisee whom Jesus had healed of leprosy. It was in Bethany, the town of Christ's devoted followers Martha, Mary, and Lazarus. Its inhabitants were making quite a big deal out of the Nazarene rabbi; they sensed his ministry was heading toward a climax at Jerusalem. Word had spread among the crowds making pilgrimage toward the holy city that one of Jesus' followers had at one time been a corpse. Everyone wanted to see the man, and his healer.

In this tense excitement, Simon hoped to honor the great teacher and give him a restful Friday evening. All was proceeding as planned, with Jesus and Lazarus reclining in honored places, when suddenly the guest room filled with a pungent fragrance. The nostrils of Judas were the first to identify and quantify it: pure nard, very expensive. He and others dropped their bread when they saw that a woman named Mary had crept in and was pouring an alabaster vial of the perfume on Jesus' head. Then she removed his sandals, rubbed his dust-streaked feet with the remainder of the nard, and wiped them off with her hair.

Judas did some quick calculating. That was three hundred days' wages evaporating into thin air. Noting the disturbed look on the faces around him, he declared that this perfume might have been sold for a good price and the proceeds placed in his fund—for the poor, of course. Most of the disciples agreed; it did seem a waste.

They were even more disturbed that a mere woman should be so forward. Was it really proper for her to be anointing the spotless rabbi? What business did she have interrupting their pleasant evening?

It's customary to rush to the defense of this woman, of course. Everybody's ganging up on her. But let's take a moment to think about what she was trailing along with her, besides that fragrance. Mary was pretty messed up. She'd gone about as far down as you could go in that society: prostitution. She'd had some tough breaks, but surely had blown chance after chance to have a better life. She may well have been the Mary from whom Jesus cast out seven demons. That's a lot of addictions or dysfunctions or crises. That's a repeat offender.

Think about life with a person like this when the perfume wears off, a person whose impulses keep getting her into trouble. Mary's the one you need to draw careful boundaries around. *Don't let the disorder of your life overwhelm mine. Don't try to make me responsible for your disasters.*

These are the kind of people who badly need order and discipline in their lives. It's such a temptation to try to control them. Hey, they need controlling. Others are always pleading with them: If you could just be a little more considerate. If you could just be on time for once. If you would just call when you say you're going to call. If you would clean up after yourself.

Interestingly enough, many disciplined individuals marry people who are a little out of control. Opposites attract. Spontaneity seems refreshing. But after the initial chemistry wears down, opposites start to jar. Off-the-cuff Sam comes home to inform his by-the-book wife, Melissa, that he's just invited ten buddies over for the Monday night game and some snacks. Let's have a party!

Melissa instantly freezes as she's placing a can of peas in the pantry—in alphabetical order of course, before plums. How could Sam do this to her? "Just a few snacks? Do you have any idea what this entails?!"

Melissa has to plan everything ahead of time. She knows how many toothpicks there are in the house, for pity's sake, so unexpected guests are like death threats in the mail.

Human nature being what it is, Sam and Melissa often push each other to extremes. Sam becomes more and more spontaneous to make up for how uptight Melissa is. She needs to lighten up. Melissa becomes more and more controlled to make up for how disorganized Sam is.

It happens in a work environment as well. A disciplined boss will give a loose-cannon employee more and more projects to keep him on track. Follow procedure! The spontaneous employee will come up with crazier and crazier ideas, and get further and further behind, trying to make up for the rut his unimaginative boss is in.

Simon, like most Pharisees, had gone to great lengths to keep publicans and prostitutes from contaminating his life with their chaos. His religion protected him from promiscuous contact by making him untouchable. So of course he didn't like the intrusion of the woman with the perfume.

Several voices around him joined in Judas' criticism. Some reprimanded Mary directly. Her face flushed. She was about to beat a hasty retreat when Jesus silenced the guests with a sharp rebuke: "Leave her alone." And then he proceeded to show a Master's touch. He understood something about people who are blown this way and that by their impulses and emotions. He knew something about people who make multiple mistakes of the heart. They possess hidden treasure. They have something precious to give, something that the most disciplined and controlled of us need very badly. They have a wealth of devotion bouncing around inside.

Jesus told Simon a story about two debtors. One owed ten times as much as the other. If a banker cancels both debts, Jesus asked, which one of them will love him more?

Simon admitted, "I suppose the one who had the bigger debt canceled."

Jesus turned toward the embarrassed woman and told everyone how graciously she'd treated him. She'd been the consummate hostess, doing much more than the well-meaning Simon. She'd taken the customary kiss of greeting and the washing of feet to a whole new level, and had done it very humbly. Her awkward act flowed out of genuine love and admiration. Simon, like everyone else in the room, just didn't know what to do before this wealth of affection. He didn't see the hidden treasure in it.

Jesus noticed. "She wet my feet with her tears. She has not stopped kissing my feet. She loves much. Her many sins have been forgiven." All those frowning in unison had their lives much more together than this immoral female. But they were missing something essential. Jesus summed up their lives in one startling comment: the one who has been forgiven little, loves little.

In this scene we discover yet another thing that turns to gold, with the right touch: affection. We need to honor affection. Too often it goes unnoticed. Yes, it's often overdone or misplaced or sloppy. It sometimes embarrasses us. It's often an interruption in busy, efficient lives. But even in it's messiest form, affection is something we ignore at our peril.

Affection is the splash that invites us into the deep pool.
Affection is the wind that makes us want to salute the flag.

Affection is the fluff that makes the cake a cake.

Affection is the accident that trumps well-laid plans.

Affection pours dreams into the humdrum.

Affection disarms well-rehearsed accusations.

Affection jump-starts ways to stay together.

Affection short-circuits reasons to drift apart.

Affection sings where duty nags.

One of the reasons Jesus touched affection so skillfully was that he remained touchable. He didn't heal from a distance. He got up close and personal. We find him putting his fingers in the ears of a deaf man. He made mud with his saliva and applied it to the eyes of a blind man. He grasped the cold hand of a dead child and lifted her up.

Jesus did these things when just a word would do. That's one way he created an intimacy with those he blessed. He touched. He was touched. As the greatest proof of his claims to be the Messiah, he didn't offer a discourse on the prophets; he asked Thomas to put his finger in the wounds on his palms and to touch the gaping scar on his side.

Jesus exposed himself to casual familiarities. That's what drove the Pharisees crazy about his spending an evening with "publicans and sinners," cheats and adulterers. And it's part of his incredible charisma.

Nineteenth-century critics who viewed William Turner's

painting "Snowstorm" damned it as mere "soapsuds and white-wash." It was too wild, too indifferent to the established canons of art. What they didn't know was that this painting came after the artist boarded a steamboat and had himself lashed to a spar during a violent storm. What he got on canvas was four terrified hours of the sea exploding around him.

Most of the time we have no idea what goes into "wild" displays of affection, no idea of the struggle, the trouble, littered in its wake. It's just soapsuds, just fluff, we say. But affection is really the picture worth a thousand well-intentioned words.

We would do well to appreciate the art, even when it comes from the "unworthy." The woman with the illicit perfume had hidden treasure for the disciples. She was fast of heart where they were slow of heart to believe. She poured it all out, no reservation, where they hesitated to commit, to reflect Christ's love back. She would become one of his most devoted followers. They would snore through his ordeal in the Garden of Gethsemane.

Affection leaks out of cracked hearts. It doesn't have a proper time or place. It's a gesture you'd better grab right in the air, like a butterfly. It lights on your shoulder then it's gone—if you don't trap it with a gift in kind.

We push people away who have this hidden treasure. They mess up the furniture; they spill the coffee. They're also spilling something we need to soak up. So instead of just building boxes for their loose lives, we can open our own hand; we can be touchable.

Too many of us do works of charity by the numbers. Our self-less gestures seem memorized. We break love down into component parts. We domesticate it in church services and devotionals.

But love also exists in the wild. So when you come on it suddenly, don't make it skittish; don't make it run away. Find the hidden treasure. It's waiting there in the very person you are flabbergasted with. It's bubbling up in the individual you're trying to get to pipe down.

When Marilyn walks in the door, it's like the sun jumping out from behind a cloud. All the colors come to life again. She's one of those cheery, good-hearted individuals who makes unconditional love seem as simple as falling off a chair. And I have the amazing good fortune to be married to her.

But on this day, as she tossed her car keys on the kitchen counter and excitedly showed me a couple of things she'd picked up at the mall, I felt very conditional. I grunted approval at the bright blouses. I smiled faintly as she told me what a bargain they were. I turned back to my laptop as she commented on how beautiful the queen palms looked outside the window.

The fact is, I'd been stewing all morning. I'd been rehearsing my complaints about *Mosby's Medical Dictionary* and *Basic Skills and Procedures*. They were some of the heavy volumes that *still* lay scattered on our den rug. How long was it going to take this woman to put them away in the cabinets? It had been two weeks! She kept saying she was going to get around to it. But her old textbooks from nursing school were still there, scarring the perfect landscape of our family room.

Different relationships reveal different things about who you really are. In my marriage I've discovered I can get quite uptight about little things, which is unsettling, because I always thought I was this laid-back, spontaneous, free-spirited guy. Okay, maybe that was just high school. Anyway, I'm more disciplined and orderly now than Marilyn. She's the impulsive one. She's adorable. And she's making me crazy.

So while I was sitting at my desk with the laptop, pounding out wonderful words about the grace of God, dark accusations kept rushing through my head. She spends hours at the mall, but can't take five minutes to put her %*&+!* books away. I'm working my butt off here all day, fixing sack lunches for the kids at night, and she hasn't even finished the laundry! Maybe instead of sleeping in, she could lift a little finger . . .

Such tiny irritants can create a whole list of District Attorney questions. You know the drill.

Marilyn is, in fact, anything but a slouch. She takes care of business quite well, thank you. But she doesn't always do it in my time frame and in the order I'd like. Being the more disciplined one, I want to *make* her more efficient, *make* her accomplish more. And my inability to control the details of Marilyn's life angers me. I can't make her exactly like me.

That's what I had been building up all morning when Miss Sunshine walked through the door.

There have been many times when I've shoved my dark mood in her face and watched as the light is erased from her eyes. I accuse her. I complain. I build a huge case for my great suffering out of some little annoyance. And Marilyn listens. Her eagerness to please makes it all too easy for me to keep complaining.

But this afternoon when she asked me what was wrong and put her arms around my neck, I decided to do what I'd often wanted to do before. I accepted her embrace. I hugged back. I told her what a precious sweetheart she is. She breathed out a reply and I felt the wealth of her affection wash through me. I felt how wonderful it is to be loved by a healthy person. It cleansed me. It made the nursing textbooks small again.

Just glancing at my married life I can see that so much turns on this one choice I have. I can either fret over the fact that things aren't exactly as I want them to be, or I can receive the hidden treasure of this woman's affection.

So often we can go one way or the other—especially those of us who think we've got our act together, our schedule down, our priorities straight, our chores crossed off. We can miss out on the very reward of all our efforts. We can pass off on the one thing that all our efficiency is supposed to make room for.

I want to touch like Jesus touched. I want to develop that skill. I want to bless back. And one way we can bless back is to give meaning to random acts of affection. We can frame them. That's something the more disciplined can often give back to the more spontaneous. Our reflective side can bring out the true colors in their bright side.

Jesus did that for the woman who poured perfume on his feet. He didn't just spotlight the great devotion behind her gesture. Matthew, Mark, and John show that he immortalized her act by linking it to his coming passion. "She poured perfume on my body beforehand to prepare for my burial," he said. Jesus was about to place himself in the hands of his enemies, endure a mock trial, suffer greatly on the cross, agonize even more in the darkness of separation from his Father, and then lie cold and bloodless in a tomb. The climactic confrontation of his life was approaching. But his disciples couldn't grasp it all. They offered no real companionship during that most difficult of journeys toward Jerusalem.

But in Simon's house Jesus transformed this woman's impulsive act into a companion piece, a part of the spectacle of his atonement. Jesus seems to say, "Only this woman, among you all, has echoed ultimate truth. Only she is identified with me in the great ordeal ahead."

Jesus lifted up Mary's act as an emblem for all the redeemed down through the ages who would come to honor his sacrifice with twenty-twenty hindsight as much as she honored it in the moment, from the heart. She heard these wonderful words: "Wherever the gospel is preached throughout the world, what she has done will also be told, in memory of her." Jesus honored the dishonored one by giving her meaning. It's his insight into the significance of her gesture that redeems her from the shadows. Mary can take home her alabaster vial, now fittingly empty, and walk tall amid the gossips of Bethany. She is part of the Messiah's sacrifice; no one will ever take that away from her.

Each one of us can turn affection to gold. Touch back. Give meaning. Show them how valuable their accidental grace is. Show them nothing is wasted. Show them it's part of the magical touch of Christ.

Cited:

Jesus and Mary—John 12:2-11; Mark 14:1-9

Leave her alone—Mark 14:6

Bigger debt—Luke 7:43

THE FLICKER OF FAITH

THE BITS of branch and dried mud falling on his head in that crowded room surely must have been annoying. The noise of four men furiously digging through the roof overhead must have been distracting. After all, Jesus was revealing the essence of the kingdom of heaven. But the intruders just wouldn't stop the hacking. And finally, following another downpour of debris, a mat descended toward the small opening in the crowd where Jesus stood. On it stretched a desperately sick man.

Jesus could have seen a lot of things when he squinted up at the bright patch of blue and saw the men in silhouette braced against the roof beams, lowering this figure with ropes. He could have seen rudeness and insensitivity. He could have spotted presumption. He could have identified pathetic desperation. He could have noted the men's obvious impatience.

Instead, Matthew, Mark, and Luke all tell us that Jesus saw their faith. Standing in an impromptu shaft of light in which the dirt and leaves still floated down, that's what he focused on.

Jesus—as the celebrity healer passing through town—could have noticed a lot of things as he was jostled around in the middle of Capernaum. He could have acknowledged all the fans trying to touch him so they could tell their grandchildren they had (that is, if this guy should live long enough to really become famous). Instead Jesus froze the wild procession mid-stride and demanded to know who the one person was who had reached out to touch him — in faith. That pale, embarrassed woman over there slinking back into the crowd. Yes, that was the one. He'd sensed a brush of faith and wanted her to know that's what healed her.

Jesus had a nose for faith. He always emphasized it. Nothing made him happier than finding it. Nothing perplexed him more than the lack of it. He never tired of telling people it was their faith that had made them well. And he could spot it in the most unlikely places.

A pushy blind man by the side of the road won't stop yelling. Jesus sees faith.

A Canaanite woman begs pathetically. Jesus sees faith.

The village prostitute interrupts a dignified gathering to sob over the Master's feet. Jesus sees faith.

One out of ten deliriously happy lepers has the presence of mind to do the polite thing. Sent on his way with a clean bill of health, he turns back and thanks the Master. Jesus sees faith.

What stands out about Christ building his kingdom on faith is that he was quite willing to start with the barest of materials. He took whatever stray bits of faith came his way—and did wonders with them.

This is something that often gets lost in the shuffle of most religious organizations. After all, the Christian faith has been precisely defined and carefully structured for two thousand years. So believers are often afraid to endorse anything that isn't a full acknowledgment of correct doctrine. *Let's not water down the faith. Let's not put our stamp on spacey notions of God or on hazy theories of the atonement.*

Well, wanting to keep Christian beliefs clear is understandable. But too often we confuse the end with the beginning. Most church groups have a nice, tidy doctrinal package you're supposed to sign onto when you "come in faith." Belief is supposed to turn on after you've studied over the package and concluded that this is, in fact, the whole truth and nothing but the truth.

But that's where a journey of faith takes you. That's the destination. Too often we don't affirm faith as much as ideology. Faith becomes black or white. You either have it or you don't. You're either walking on that lighted path or slipping away into outer darkness.

Many of my friends have been turned off to organized religion for that reason. It's about a checklist, and they're on a journey.

Jesus, however, made it a point to affirm faith the moment he sniffed it out. And he affirmed all kinds of faith: The superstitious faith of the woman in the crowd who thought there might be a bit of magic in the edge of Jesus' cloak. The pleading half-faith of the man whose son lay convulsing on the ground. The terrified faith of a synagogue official whose twelve-year-old daughter lay dying.

What did people in Capernaum and Bethesda and Jerusalem come to Jesus with? They usually came with, "Who is this guy?" They came with prejudices. They came with idle curiosity and with terrible desperation. They came because of rumors and half-truths. They came with blank stares. Very few came to him with a clear understanding of Jesus the Messiah.

But Jesus managed to touch faith. He awakened it as a living thing. It's a process, not a piece of equipment with neat component parts. Jesus wasn't afraid to endorse the first stumbling steps, the first flicker of faith. He had the touch. He could get that dimly burning wick to burst into flame.

Faith can't be forced. It can't be argued into being. If new believers are like babies in the faith, too many religious people want to stuff food into those incoherent gurgles. Give her steak. Define justification and sanctification and tell me how and when the Spirit comes down. The church hovers around these babies, unable to resist the impulse to dress them up in the right doctrines and show them off to relatives.

Better to treat faith like a shy lover. Don't come on too strong.

Faith is a guess instead of a shrug.
Faith is a spark when you've never seen a fire.
Faith is an empty hand that feels something dropped
   into it.

Faith is a decision to keep looking.

Faith is accepting fullness elsewhere because there's
emptiness in your heart.

Faith is getting dressed up because you have somewhere
to go.

Jesus' touch teases out faith, like a child's smile. Give it a little space. Relax. Stop wringing your hands over someone's fuzzy grasp of the truth. Faith is loose out there, ricocheting off New Age crystals and tired church rituals and dead-end philosophies, and it's bound to hit the gospel at some point. Cheer it on. Believe that it will turn more fully toward its author and perfecter. Drop morsels here and there. Share a little; listen a lot.

Faith doesn't typically arrive at the head of a parade, banners blowing, trumpets blaring. In fact, it can seem such an intangible thing that many people don't know how to get it going. Where do you start?

The good news is that human beings already possess what God requires. We have the only thing we need for starters. Right now each one of us is investing our faith in all kinds of things. We have faith in family or country, in love or beauty. We believe the sun will come up tomorrow. We trust close friends. The ingredients are already there in our hearts. We don't have to build faith from scratch. We just have to direct it toward Mr. Right. God will show us, in time, why he is the best place for our faith.

That's why it's good for all of us to catch stray bits of faith and celebrate them. It may just be a pause in a list of doubts. It may just be a flicker of joy across the face of a confirmed pessimist. It may just be someone's admission that they don't have all the answers.

But spy out faith. Sense the unspoken desire to believe in someone flailing between all the horror and all the glory in the world. (Why let horror have the last word?)

Feel the trust struggling to be born in a cry of anger against God. (You don't quarrel with someone who's not there.)

All our struggles are working toward a wonderful punch line: when your faith turns to God, it turns to gold, it becomes a treasure. In the kingdom economy, faith isn't a consolation prize. It isn't just neediness or rolling the dice. It's the stuff miracles are made of. So we dare not turn up our noses when it knocks faintly on the door.

Jesus' wonderful touch, when it comes to faith, is based on one great principle: God's faith always precedes ours. God has said, "I believe in you," long before anyone says that back to him. Count on it.

Jesus expressed God's faith in us. That comes across in his relationship with the disciples—from beginning to end. He expressed a great deal of faith in his motley crew at the start when he promised to make them fishers of men. It was also the last gift he gave to the Twelve at his ascension.

Just before Christ's dramatic departure, the disciples dropped a bombshell of a question: "Lord, are you at this time going to restore the kingdom to Israel?" Right there, Christ could have thrown up his hands. Hadn't they been listening to anything he'd said the last three years? I'm leaving the kingdom to *you guys*!

Instead Jesus expressed faith. He answered the question simply by telling them that the Father was in charge of times and dates. And then he spoke this final blessing: "You will receive power when the Holy Spirit comes on you; and you will be my witnesses in Jerusalem, and in all Judea and Samaria, and to the ends of the earth."

God's faith is a promise instead of a question.
God's faith is a fire when we've got a spark.
God's faith is pouring it all out when no one has yet
    opened a hand.
God's faith is a decision to keep asking.
God's faith is an aching in the heart when there's
    emptiness elsewhere.
God's faith is a removal of the garments of divinity
    because he has somewhere to go.

God's faith always precedes our own. His faith in us inspires faith. His trust creates ours. Out in our lonely little boats over the deep blue sea of life's mysteries, we decide to put up a sail. It's usually a small one at first. But why not? We decide to hoist it to the top of the mast. And suddenly we realize there's wind everywhere. The sail fills up. We're moving. There's this presence filling the whole sky that wasn't tangible before. Gradually, we put up more and more sail until we're in a clipper ship slashing across the waves.

It started with some yellowed poems Genie laid out on the coffee table in her mother's Charleston home.* This was a way to change the subject. God had crept into the lively conversation she and Ellen were having. The two old friends back in their hometown had a lot of catching up to do. But Genie had discovered, to her dismay, that Ellen was now a Christian who took all that stuff about sin and Jesus and the cross very seriously. Genie couldn't imagine such things fitting her lifestyle as she fast-tracked her way to the top of entertainment writing in Chicago. At thirty-three, she'd already produced some very popular shows.

So she dragged out some old poems she'd written at the starry-eyed age of twenty-three. Ellen had expressed a keen interest in Genie's career, and poetry is where Genie's fascination with words had begun.

Ellen read over a few carefully and smiled appreciatively.

---

*This story is recorded by Eugenia Price in *The Burden Is Light!* (Westwood, N.J.: Revell, 1955).

She read others and teared up. That was odd, Genie thought, because those were the lines she'd intended to be witty and amusing. At length Ellen looked up at Genie with her big brown eyes and said, as though this had never been true of anyone else, "Love is really important to you, isn't it?"

To Genie, it seemed like an accusation, and she shook it off.

But Ellen saw even more. "You won't like this," she remarked sheepishly, "but I find in your poetry a big, wide God-hunger."

Genie laughed. They did some more catching up and Ellen said goodnight. After Ellen left, Genie couldn't escape the feeling that this girl understood her writing better than she did herself. Staring down at the crinkled pages, she realized the poems were now jumping out with things she hadn't intended to say at all.

Genie saw her a few more times before Ellen had to go back to work in New York City. It was a pity, Genie thought, such a talented, attractive young woman had gone so religious. Maybe she could help. So she started corresponding.

In her replies, Ellen didn't speak of God unless Genie brought up the subject. And she refrained from quoting the Bible, which Genie appreciated. But Ellen did talk about what she'd noticed. "Remember, I did see another 'you' begin to emerge, and I don't believe anything can stop 'her' now. This new thing isn't something that you have. It is something that has you."

Genie was intrigued, in spite of herself. Work was great in

Chicago, but it could be very lonely. In time Ellen persuaded her to come out to New York for a visit.

On the trip, a revelation struck Genie out of nowhere. Staring out the train window at the blue sky, she suddenly *knew* life did not end here.

Genie checked into the Gramercy Park Hotel and called her friend. Ellen chatted up a couple of French restaurants in the neighborhood they should visit. Genie said she now believed in another life.

"That's wonderful," Ellen replied.

"Is it wonderful? I think maybe I'm losing my mind."

A few days later Genie found herself reading the Gideon Bible from the hotel nightstand. Ellen had remarked weeks before that the way she gave old words new meanings reminded her of the prophet Ezekiel. Genie found Ezekiel in the index and read a few chapters. To her great surprise, the language blew right through her. Descriptions of an ancient temple actually made her weep—in the same way the music of Wagner and Beethoven used to hurt her blissfully.

But Genie was fighting it too. One evening, while glancing through the neighboring book of Isaiah, she came across the word "saved" and slammed the Bible shut. She hated the word. It recalled intense, dreary people who stood on street corners and passed out ugly tracts. They were forever in the business of saving souls. People with inexcusably bad taste talked about being "saved."

Genie would share her doubts and fears with Ellen. Sometimes she was downright rude, making fun because Ellen didn't drink, saying, "I could never, ever live like you do. Can anyone past the age of eight actually keep the Ten Commandments? I couldn't possibly spend the rest of my life surrounded by gloomy church people."

But Ellen never blanched, never backed away. She just kept encouraging her to read more. She believed in the faith that was growing inside her friend, kicking and screaming to get out. She affirmed every little step she made toward God and finally she suggested Genie talk to him directly.

"Me talk to God? Why, that's praying!"

"Yes, I know it is."

But one sleepless night Genie got out of bed and decided to read Scripture to the ceiling with all her heart. She couldn't pray, but that might shake something loose. It did. Some time after reading about the hand of God that fashioned her and the face that shines down on his servants, she collapsed by her hotel bed and began weeping. She began repeating a one-word prayer over and over. Just his name.

It was a dramatic encounter, but it was just the beginning. Genie didn't blossom into the faith like a flower in time-lapse. She lurched. She played hide-and-seek. She could blurt out to Ellen, "I'd give anything if I had never begun to believe in God! I'm coming apart at the seams."

Genie's faith wavered. Ellen's didn't. She kept reassuring her friend that God was up to something wonderful. Genie could still try to get over a church service with a double Scotch. But Ellen kept believing Jesus would catch on big time.

He did. Genie finally let her faith get loose and she fell into a steady love with Christ. Eugenia Price would go on to become, with her *Unshackled* drama program, the most beloved writer in Christian radio.

Cited:

Sick man through roof—Matthew 9:1-8; Mark 2:1-12; Luke 5:17-26

Woman in the crowd—Luke 8:42-48

Pushy blind man—Mark 10:52

A Canaanite woman—Matthew 15:28

A woman interrupts—Luke 7:50

Happy leper—Luke 17:19

Superstitious faith—Mark 5:27-28

Desperate faith—Mark 9:24

Terrified faith—Luke 8:49-50

Restore the kingdom—Acts 1:6

Be my witnesses—Acts 1:8

THE DIRTY TRUTH

ONE EVENING during the Passover season, Jesus' inner circle got to talking. They generated what they thought was an intense theological debate on the nature of Christ's kingdom. The Master's rather plain statements on the subject needed fleshing out. Just how would it be organized, they wondered, or more specifically, how would they, its designated heirs, organize it?

No one wanted to compete with Christ as head of state, of course, but what about those nice little vice-presidential slots? They didn't want to be pushy, but, after all, somebody had to occupy them. In those days the yen for an executive suite was expressed as a hint that a seat at the right or left hand of the Master would be greatly appreciated.

The disciples continued their debate as they walked down the narrow, crowded streets of Jerusalem toward a certain upper room. That's where thousands of years of Passover remembrances would be given a new substance. That night would create a historic crossroad where two covenants would meet, intertwine for a few moments, and then exchange the sacred burden of meaning forever.

But the disciples couldn't see this coming. They were too busy hammering out the details of their relative status. Who would be greatest in the coming kingdom? Andrew and John could stake claim to being the first to follow Christ, making the transition from disciples of John the Baptist to the One pointed out as the "Lamb of God." Peter might interject (as the usual leader of the discussion) that he was first to "really" follow the Master, leaving behind his fishing business once and for all, there by the Sea of Galilee. But others could quickly point out that they were called on the very same day and made the same decision to become fishers of men. And Judas, clearing his throat, could argue that the one in charge of finances for the group merited serious consideration.

The chosen Twelve laid out their qualifications more and more heatedly. And slowly, word by word, claim by claim, the fabric of their discipleship unraveled. As they climbed the stairs to the rented room, old jealousies and resentments trailed them like Pharisee spies. They reclined on pillows by the table, kicked off their sandals, and realized that no servant was there to perform the chore of washing everyone's feet; not a soul felt moved to fetch some water. They eyed each other accusingly, wanting someone to blame for the bad feelings each felt guilty about.

The pitcher, basin, and towel accented the silence. No one moved to touch them. No one spoke. They pretended the animosity filling the room like a bad smell just wasn't there.

Jesus had been deep in thought, contemplating the traumatic events just ahead. But now he looked around and saw what everyone was ignoring. So he decided to stop history. He put the establishment of his Passover sacrament on pause, refusing to go on with beautiful words about his broken body and shed blood while ugly feelings cut at the people he loved.

Rising from his place, the Master slowly wrapped a towel around his waist and poured water from pitcher to basin. He moved with deliberation, but not reluctance. Every eye in the room followed his steps, every ear heard the water splashing, filling the basin, and it sounded to them like an ocean. Jesus then knelt down and washed the streets of Jerusalem from his disciples' feet. He washed the toes of John, first to come to him, yes. He washed Judas, renowned financier. He washed Peter, dynamic leader who had sacrificed everything, and Nathaniel, great intellectual, and Philip, who had told Nathaniel in the first place, and James, whose mother had first put in a bid for him for the right-hand position.

Jesus washed the feet of all these great luminaries—and the ocean swept over them. They saw who it was there draped in a soiled towel and they saw their pettiness for what it was. Decades later John would remember with a pang: "Knowing that the Father had given all things into His hands, and that He had come forth from God, and was going back to God . . . He poured water into the basin, and began to wash the disciples' feet."

What Jesus was doing in that Upper Room was dealing with dirt. He got his hands dirty. He acted the part of a servant, but he did so in a very special way, in a way that made his friends confront the ugliness no one wanted to talk about. That was part of his remarkable touch. It was yet another reason he was able to find so much hidden treasure.

Jesus knew when and how to deal with the dirty truth. He tried to get Peter to spot that strand of over-confidence, that lack of reflection, which was going to send him sprawling during the midnight trial. "You will disown me three times." Those were very hard words to say to the natural leader of the group. But they needed to be said. Peter wasn't looking at the hard facts about himself.

Jesus didn't pretend the woman at the well could just chugalug on the Water of Life without confronting her past. He didn't ignore her five husbands out of politeness. He gently helped her realize she needed a whole new start.

There are a lot of things people would just rather not talk about. And sometimes there are things eating away at us and tearing at relationships, which we can't for the life of us talk about. We desperately need to hide the dirt. We're afraid it will only do more damage out in the open.

Well, there's actually a good reason we're afraid. We're afraid because my secrets are bad news, but your secrets are great gossip. What we hate telling about ourselves is exactly what we love revealing about others. Your spouse's affair can't be hidden too carefully; the neighbor's affair is the best thing that ever happened to your Tuesday morning coffee circle.

Counselors and mental health professionals have been preaching honesty for many decades now. It's one of the keys to healing. You've got to open your heart or the wounds will fester and make you sick. Don't just put on your I'm-okay façade of competence with your peers. Don't just put on a smiley face at church. Be authentic.

Well, guess what. After you've spilled your guts and then found the news e-mailed to all your friends, a mask begins to make a lot of sense. Silence seems the better part of valor.

People talk. And people talk most about the scandals, the missteps. Human nature hears, "You shouldn't repeat gossip." It responds, "Okay, I'll say this only once."

This is our predicament. We dig up everyone's dirt but our own. We need to open up, but we're afraid of the consequences.

And that's why Jesus' touch with his quarrelsome disciples is so refreshing and enlightening. He dealt with the dirt without spreading a word. He exposed their hidden animosities without a single rebuke. His actions spoke loud enough.

Jesus dealt with the problem directly, and privately. He was fleshing out one of his great relationship principles: "If your brother sins against you, go and show him his fault, just between the two of you. If he listens to you, you have won your brother over."

This is Christ's one-sentence antidote to destructive gossip. Is there a problem? Talk it over "just between the two of you." Don't phone friends "for advice." Don't "gather more facts" in the neighborhood. Don't create a website to tell your side of the story.

Instead, the Man with the Golden Touch says, Get some face time; go to the source. Do that first. Ask questions. Share your feelings. The vast majority of problems dissipate just because someone bothers to find out where the other person is coming from.

Being direct can be hard. Sometimes that's the last person you want to speak with. Maybe he really has been unfair. Maybe you think she richly deserves all the gossip she gets.

But try to imagine this: What if God had a habit of talking trash? What if gossip was one of the divine attributes, along with omniscience and omnipotence? I'm sure he's got plenty of tidbits to pass along, secrets he's spied out from his eye-in-the-sky vantage point. That heavenly satellite can take some amazingly good close-ups—of the innermost heart. The Lord could keep an awful lot of angels entertained for an awfully long time.

He'd get a lot of mileage just glancing at a few church bulletins. Think of how these items that have appeared of late might look.

Amazing Insults

Low Self-Esteem Support Group will meet Thursday at 8 P.M. Please use the back door.

At the evening service tonight, the sermon topic

will be "What is Hell?" Come early and listen to our
choir practice.

Scandals Brewing

This evening at 7 P.M. there will be a hymn sing in the
park across from the Church. Bring a blanket and
come prepared to sin.

For those of you who have children and don't
know it, we have a nursery downstairs.

Simply Outrageous

Bertha Belch, a missionary from Africa, will be speak-
ing tonight at the Calvary Memorial Church in Racine.
Come tonight and hear Bertha Belch all the way from
Africa.

Think about it. Maybe the insult is a misprint. Maybe the scan-
dal is mostly imagined.

We can all be thankful God's not a gossip. Instead he prom-
ises those who open up to him that he will throw their transgres-
sions into the depths of the sea; he will wipe all embarrassments
off the record; he will make crimson stains white as snow.

God's not a gossip, because he's into good news. He's about
grace. That's what the eye in the sky is all about. He's seeing a
lot of dirt. But he's sifting through it for nuggets of gold. That

perspective will make all the difference in our relationships.

When Jesus knelt at his disciples' feet and put his hands in the muddy water, he was looking for something better than the ugly thing that filled the room. He was looking for men who would become leaders by becoming servants. He was looking for men who would change the world because they tasted grace.

And that's exactly what he found. He found hidden treasure in those quarrelsome disciples.

What are we looking for when we deal with dirt? That makes all the difference. Are we just spreading mud around, or are we digging through ore? Gossip stops when looking for hidden treasure starts.

In confronting the dirty truth,

You can dig through anger and come to genuine
    affection.
You can sift through piles of misunderstanding and
    suddenly find a close bond on your hands.
You can apply a little direct pressure to accusations and
    discover respect sparkling at your feet.
You can carefully turn up the heat on alienation and see
    a hard face melting into an embrace.

So yes, go to the person you have a problem with. But don't go looking to prove him wrong. Don't go looking to gather evidence.

Go looking to clear it up, because there just might be a treasure waiting for you. That's Christ's gracious way of dealing with dirt. He understood the alchemy that can turn it into gold.

One sleepless night in the August humidity of Osaka, Japan, I began processing all my dirt on Joe. I was in my second year teaching English and Bible at a Christian language school. My roommates were still adjusting to the challenge of communicating their faith in an unfamiliar culture. I had come to think of myself as a wise veteran who had to put up with the cultural illiteracy of newcomers.

Joe seemed the typical short-termer—flitting from one exotic "experience" to another. He always managed to swing light class schedules, top-of-the-line stereo equipment, and female tour guides. I spent a lot of time preparing for my Bible classes and thought I was finally getting a foothold in the deeply secular minds of my students. Joe seemed content just repeating church clichés.

My complaints had been building for weeks and now they blustered through my head as I tossed and turned. Here it is after eleven and Joe's still out goofing off. And he was supposed to be so tired tonight he couldn't make it through all of his English drills. Some teacher. The guy's already four lessons behind. He's always late for staff meetings and then has to read letters when we're trying to get things done. I wonder if he's really here or back in California with the "absolute doll" he spends all his time writing to.

The thing that probably irritated me most about Joe and my other roommates was how little they tried to adapt to their new environment. They were always whining about having to eat with chopsticks or having to take off their shoes at the doorway. And then there was the *ofuro*.

Our Japanese-style bath heater had to be carefully regulated. I had to constantly watch lest they turn on the heater without filling the tub, or turn on the gas without a flame, or, as seemed to happen all the time, leave the thing on for the next guy— who never came.

Joe's shortcomings seemed to litter the apartment we shared like his audio gadgets. I was always running into them. They made our conversation over breakfast and supper short and one-sided. He talked; I grunted. I didn't want to bring up all the dirt. I was much too loving a Christian for such pettiness. I just let it drone on and on in my head—like a certain faint rumbling sound that barely registered that night as I tried to sleep.

The next morning I dragged myself out of bed and managed to find a little soup in the kitchen. Joe came in looking chipper; he had the funniest story to tell. He'd come in around one in the morning (no kidding) and heard a gurgling and splashing some-where in the house. Opening the bathroom door, he lurched back as a thick cloud of steam poured into the hallway. Joe could hardly see or breathe, but he managed to feel his way to the gas switch and turn off the *ofuro* heater.

He was chuckling as he told me this. The boiling water quieted. The steam cleared. He peered cautiously inside. The rubber mat that covered our tub had been warped into a saddle shape by the intense heat. But we hadn't blown ourselves up.

It was then that something hit me right between the eyes. It was *me*. Mother Mosley had left the *ofuro* on full blast from 10:00 P.M. to 1:00 A.M. That was the faint rumbling sound.

But Joe wasn't finished. He also had a great story to tell about how Junko had opened up.

Junko? Wasn't she the student he was always drooling over?

As it turned out, that night she'd had some tough questions about God. She'd prayed about something very important and God had answered no. It didn't seem the response of a merciful Lord at all.

So Joe gave her a few examples about how God had guided him in the past. Sometimes a no turns out to be a good answer. He shared how God had helped him get around some roadblocks in his life. As a result, that divine will was now something he could trust. He could even trust God about the girl back home he was crazy about. He was praying that God's will would be done.

That blew Junko away. She couldn't believe anyone could give something like that up to God. And Joe had the thrill of seeing this often-perplexed student break through to a new acceptance of God's big plan for her.

I dropped my chopsticks (that I'd been skillfully wielding

over a bowl of rice) and leaned back in the chair. It was time to do more than grunt. I had to get the dirt out, but it wasn't the dirt I'd counted on.

I told Joe who was behind all that steam billowing into the hallway. I also told him I'd tried to answer Junko's questions several times in Bible classes. I'd discoursed at great length on God's will. But I wasn't getting through. And now the guy who seems to be out messing around . . .

Joe and I had a great breakfast. Our first. It would lead to many other surprising conversations. I was forced to see hidden treasure where I'd only wanted to criticize. I didn't have sense enough to get the dirt out face to face on my own. It had taken an *ofuro* near-disaster to make me do it. But I'm very glad we cleared things up. You can see so much better when you're not secretly processing your complaints into a lot of hot air.

Cited:

Washing the disciples' feet—John 13 (NASB, NIV)
Brother sins against you—Matthew 18:15

SEVEN

THOSE HOPELESS CASES

T HE NEIGHBORS had stopped whatever they were doing to join the procession, so it was quite large as it moved past the gates of the city, in honor of the widow who'd lost her only son. Soon, however, this funeral collided with an even larger procession coming into Nain, one that seemed like a parade. It was an awkward moment. The parade included the noise of the formerly dumb and the agility of the formerly lame. It throbbed with the energy of those Jesus had just healed. Now laughter had to die down quickly to respectful silence.

But Jesus didn't just step aside to let the mourners pass. He made the awkward moment even worse by telling the woman, "Do not weep." Just what was she supposed to do, count her blessings?

Jesus then stepped over to the bier where a young man lay pale and cold—and touched it. Another big mistake. The bearers stopped in surprise. Touching a coffin meant, for the observant Jew, a whole day's uncleanness. Touching a corpse required a week's uncleanness. It looked like Jesus was blundering into the full seven-day quarantine as he leaned in under the shade of the palm canopy.

And then, to top off his errors that afternoon, Jesus began giving orders to the dead man. He wanted him to get up.

What happened next stopped the mourners in mid-wail. It paralyzed those tearing their garments. It froze those throwing dirt on their heads. The deceased actually sat up and began asking where he was.

That's when raw fear swept through the funeral—the instant of terror when you know you're in the presence of something outside this world. But it quickly turned to shouts of joy—for almost everyone. The Pharisees hurried off to hold a panel discussion on precisely what kind of ceremonial purification might be required of one who touched a corpse who was not in fact a corpse, but about to become a living soul. Friends and family were ecstatic. Jesus had the privilege of taking the alumnus of the grave by the hand and presenting him to his mother.

There are not too many people who see potential in a corpse. Sure, there are the jokes about the Jewish mother recommending chicken soup—"It couldn't hurt." But most of us know when to give up.

Jesus didn't. Lazarus has been dead four days? He's a decomposing body? Let's see what we can do here.

A little girl is lying there before her brokenhearted parents, lifeless as limestone? I'll go wake her up.

Jesus had a knack for taking on hopeless cases. He didn't just touch the burdened and the broken who longed for his cure. He touched those who seemed incapable of responding. He touched those paralyzed for decades by physical and psychological illnesses. He touched women who had sunk from promiscuity all the way into prostitution. He touched tax collectors who had turned "a little on the side" into a complete sellout to the Romans.

Jesus was always coming up with a plan for hopeless cases. He didn't understand that leprosy just can't be fixed. Lunatics can't be fixed. A raging storm can't be fixed. Death, above all, isn't something that's fixable. It's not reversible. But Jesus didn't get it. Even when it came to coffins, Jesus thought outside the box.

There is something we can turn to gold today just because Jesus thought it worthwhile to touch the dead. There is something we can reach out to because he set entirely new boundaries on the fixable.

Jesus brings us this conviction: there are no hopeless cases. In fact, grace and hopeless cases can't exist in the same universe. There is no fail-safe system that keeps it out. There is no impregnable wall to healing. There is no evil too potent for the cure.

Not everyone is going to respond to grace, of course. Not everyone is going to experience spiritual healing. That's clear from the way things pan out in Revelation. Some are going to cling to their alienation from God all the way to the lake of fire.

But there's hope for everyone. There's that potential, because Christ's act of redemption has covered all the bases. While we were dead in our trespasses and sins, Jesus touched us.

This is your life. This is your life on grace. Any questions?

Hope changes things. I saw a dramatic example of that while interviewing prisoners at Victor Valley Correctional Facility. It's a remarkable experiment in rehabilitation: a Christian prison. That sounds a bit bizarre. But a group of believers in Bakersfield, California, wanted to confront the culture of criminality. What if you could create a prison with a radically different environment? What if you could reinforce all the good choices?

At Victor Valley there are actually two mirror-image prisons. In order to contract with the state, and not interfere with anyone's religious freedom, the founders of Maranatha Prisons had to give inmates a choice between a conventional rehabilitation program and one run on Christian principles—both in identical facilities.

At Victor Valley I talked with many inmates who'd opted for the latter. They had few illusions about the uphill climb they faced. These weren't guys who'd run a few stoplights. They were violent, repeat felons. They had decades of the seamy side of life carved into their faces. They knew the usual prison drill. A careless word here can get a man knifed. A careless elbow there can flare into a full-scale riot. The learning curve doesn't exactly go in the right direction. As Juan told me, "Going to a usual prison, for most criminals, is like going to a convention. It's where you make a new career move. It's where you do your networking."

But these men found something powerful at Victor Valley: hope built into the system. The staff worked hard to make sure all the programs reinforced one essential idea: God's power can build new characters; he can create lasting changes.

But it wasn't just the professions of faith that hit me there inside those thick concrete walls and steel gates. Jailhouse religion isn't hard to come up with. What impressed me most was an honest struggle to deal with anger. These men were coming to grips with a cycle of rage and violence that had seeped into their bones. They were taking the steps to replace those old habits.

Vincent now catches himself giving other short-fused guys advice: "Don't take it so personal."

Austin had always been a "solid wood," sticking with his own race. Now he's "getting into God together" with blacks.

Anthony has kicked a twenty-year addiction.

I came away from Victor Valley believing that hope gave these men the leverage to do all these things.

Hope changes things. Studies have shown that hope gives people better odds of beating serious illnesses. Studies have shown that abused children who latch onto a bit of hope somewhere have a better chance of surviving, and even thriving, later.

And the good news is this: we can inject hope into any and every situation. That's the touch that Christ's interruption of the Nain procession makes possible.

Hope is the weightless sunrise that displaces the gravity
of night.

Hope is an optimist who knows more than you do.

Hope is the exception that disproves the rule.

Hope dilutes the toxic past.

Hope energizes the lethargic present.

Hope enjoys the future in advance.

Hope is shock therapy for shortsightedness.

Hope basks in the silver lining.

A lack of hope actually makes us irrational. Frail human beings, pushed by this and that, can inject hopelessness into all kinds of situations. People have committed suicide after receiving a draft notice for a dangerous war. They've started drinking to drown out their addictions. People divorce a spouse on the suspicion of unfaithfulness.

Fearing the worst, we guarantee the worst. Hopeless cases multiply. That's the way of all flesh. But Jesus reaches through all these things, through each and every obstacle—and comes up with hidden treasure. There he is, touching the dead outside Nain. Death was an absolute a few seconds ago. Jesus deconstructs it into a passing mood.

In order to see just how we can find hidden treasure in hopeless cases, it helps to distinguish Jesus' touch from what's *not* Jesus' touch. His way of relating to those "beyond the pale" contrasts with two other unhealthy ways of relating to such cases: Sometimes we touch too much. Sometimes we don't touch at all.

First, an example of the latter. There are times when we secretly want someone or some group to be a hopeless case. We want to seal them up in that category.

Many of us are indignant over abortion. Well, there's a lot to be indignant about. People routinely dispose of the unborn because those children threaten to arrive at an inconvenient time. That's a tragedy. But before we throw stones, Jesus asks us to look at our hearts. Is there something behind the reflex to put this particular sin beyond the pale? Maybe you've been celibate for years. How does it feel to see people *not* having to pay for promiscuity? You've been faithful during decades of marriage. How does it feel to see some adulterer sweep his girlfriend's unwanted pregnancy under the carpet?

Well, maybe AIDS *should* remain incurable. Maybe condoms *shouldn't* work.

It's good to ask yourself, *Is my passionate abortion protest driven by love for these lost children, or by secret resentment?* The unacknowledged desire to see a certain group punished kills hope. We lose the touch. We may say the right words, but we don't make people feel there's a way to get from where they are to grace.

Resentment kills hope. Resentment writes people off.

But looming large above all our indignation is the Christ who gives the dead orders. He reaches that far in. He creates hope out of nothing. And he tells us quite plainly that we're *all* dead in trespasses and sins. We're all in the same boat. We're all drawn into the same circle. That's why Jesus' touch can inspire us to reach out — even when we don't want to touch at all.

But there's also an opposite problem, another human limitation when it comes to hopeless cases. Sometimes we touch too much. Sometimes we need to rescue.

It's a mistake to take on hopeless cases because you need something. That kind of touch usually turns things to mud, not gold. You need the hopelessly loser boyfriend to love you. You need the hopelessly insensitive boss to be a father figure. You need the hopelessly unrepentant parent to make up for your miserable childhood. And so you keep entangling yourself in their lives. You keep finding new ways to try to make them feel obligated or guilty or concerned.

To express Jesus' touch, you can't come with a hole you're hoping to fill. Touching too much hopes for the wrong kind of miracle. You want them to change to fix *your* problem.

Jesus' touching flowed out of a healthy relationship with his heavenly Father. He was filled with the fullness of God. That intimacy overflowed to others. Jesus had so much health inside him it could even flow into corpses. He didn't need Lazarus to fill a hole in his heart or his résumé. He wanted to express something about eternal life. So he looked up to an attentive Father at the entrance of that tomb and simply asked.

Jesus' touch, the charismatic touch, the powerful touch, comes from abundance. Something spills over. This is particularly important when it comes to hopeless cases.

To avoid touching too much, start from Jesus' love. Ask, seek, knock at the right door. Christ's love will welcome us in and prepare a nourishing supper. Absorbing his love enables us to taste the fullness of the Godhead.

That's where the healthy touch starts. God fills you up. God gives you peace and satisfaction. Then you can reach out to hopeless cases. You can help people who've gone too far. You can't reassure someone who's sure they can't get back-up. You can find flickers of talent in individuals who've accepted the loser label.

Being full yourself is what propels you to believe in people who don't believe in themselves—or in anything else. You know God is up to something. You know he's still got some new trick of grace up his sleeve. You believe that he can reverse the irreversible. He's bigger than our needs.

Christ's touch finds hope in all the right places. It uncovers hidden treasure. I will always cherish my own glimpse of the length and breadth of Christ's reach.

So many tastes come back to me from my childhood meals with Adela. I can still see her vividly—rolling mashed potatoes in spicy tortillas beside the deep kitchen sink. Her bronze hands worked the cornmeal with stone mortar and pestle. She would quarter dewy mangoes and fry long thick banana slices while I loitered by the stove, growing hungry, making mischief.

Adela had come from up in the mountains of Mexico to

work as a maid in Puebla. Born from sturdy Indian stock, rooted in the soil for better and for worse, her life brimmed with labor.

She was always there. One day I thought I had been mercilessly abandoned. My parents and brothers had somehow vanished over the earth's edge (at the corner grocery store). I wept in terror on Adela's lap. And she, like a great painting animated only in the essential part, sat silent against the slow evening light of a window, calmly stroking my head.

Bored to distraction one Sunday, I grew ambitious. Why not teach Adela how to read and write? Somebody was teaching me. Adela protested of course, but my naïve enthusiasm prevailed. She pulled up a chair as I spread papers and notebook on the faded roses of our kitchen tablecloth. I printed out a few words I'd learned the week before, and she coaxed her pencil into crawling after them. I knew she could do it.

Soon, however, roller skates, marathon Monopoly, and fighting World War II with my buddy Gabrielito swallowed up the teaching career. Adela returned to her radio and solitary meditations.

Adela was someone the family prayed for, from the oldest down to me, once a week in the living room. After all, she inhabited a place where only images carried weight. She'd been hemmed in by candled saints and offerings the street dogs devoured in secret. For her, Jesus was a wooden figure bleeding paint, carried above a drunken crowd on holy days.

We prayed, but we weren't very good at talking about a

living Christ with her.

One year we left. My mother and Adela wept. I packed my best marbles and roller-skated in the patio for the last time. Adela went back up to the village where the aged can still recognize most of life. And I discovered America.

The family kept in touch. Adela would send a letter every Christmas. Down in the village square, where unclaimed animals and naked children mingled on the packed dirt, a white-shirted country gentleman always sat with his typewriter. Adela would go to him with her thoughts. Flourishing hands over the keys, he would transform the message into a flowery, formal epistle.

Through high school and college, one thing did stick with me: the prayer. It was a habit. Remember Adela. But now she was isolated in the Sierra Madre with a clump of adobe walls and a well. No word on a page could touch her. I wondered how the good news could get through. It wasn't getting through to most of my peers, even though plenty of wise teachers were trying to pound it into our privileged, rebellious heads.

I kept wondering and praying until one day I heard. It came in the faithful Christmas letter, a couple of lines that overtook me slowly. "I have become a Christian. In all my life I've never been so happy." The words sunk in. Adela? How did it happen?

There was nothing to do but send back hearty congratulations.

Adela began sending notes to me—signed in large letters by her own hand. I remembered that scrawl from the kitchen table.

And then she started sharing verses she'd read herself in the Bible. She was learning to read and write. I did my best to send encouraging verses back.

Finally there came a letter written by herself, start to finish. Phrases leaped out like fireworks. ". . . always a son to me . . . please pray for me . . . I have many great battles . . . speaking of our Lord to many . . . if we don't meet in this life . . . in heaven."

It struck me then that just maybe our ragged, unworthy petitions somehow aid God Almighty in striking home a blow of grace thousands of miles away. The world and all its troubles shrunk considerably as I sat holding those pages from the village of Cuacnopalan. It has never been the same size since.

God has ways of making himself big enough. It became impossible for me to believe that anyone is really beyond his spectacular, divine reach. It stretches out farther than I can grasp. It penetrates deeper than I can imagine. It makes hopelessness extinct. Today God is looking in the farthest, darkest corner for hidden treasure. That fact is as real to me as the hand of an Indian woman stroking my head in the slow evening light from a window.

Cited:

Funeral at Nain — Luke 7:11-17

Lazarus — John 11:43

Little girl — Mark 5:40-43

EIGHT

THE HIDDEN THIRST

EVEN THOUGH he usually gets a bad rap for tiptoeing up to Jesus in the dark, Nicodemus actually showed some courage in approaching this untrained Galilean at all. Jesus was already caught up in a deadly feud with Nicodemus's peers in the Sanhedrin. And Nicodemus had a position to maintain. He hadn't become a ruler in that august body by falling off a chair. He'd earned it—just like the Pharisees earned everything.

Was he a spy or a seeker? Nicodemus may have found himself in some no man's land between the two as he walked up the outside stairs of John's house to the guest room on the roof where Jesus was staying. But he managed a nice introduction. Tipping his hat to the miracles Jesus was alleged to have performed, he said, "We know you are a teacher who has come from God." The Pharisee was stretching it. His homeboys back at the temple knew no such thing.

Jesus sidestepped the pleasantries and went for the jugular: "You must be born again."

Nicodemus recovered enough to ask a question. How could this be true—literally? He'd trained in the study of the law, in dicing things up into black and white. He wasn't big on metaphors.

Jesus began to explain spiritual rebirth. It wasn't something that could be dissected into precepts. The Spirit, like the wind, moves invisibly, but it does move people.

Nicodemus again asked, "How can this be?" But he wasn't just playing dumb. There was a philosophical question to this born-again business to consider: how can a man first become something else in order to become something else?

Jesus then revealed his true mission and the supernatural gospel. He also focused on our human response to this gospel and what it says about our motives. What we're attracted to, what we hate—these reveal much about the moral state of our hearts.

Nicodemus probably wanted more than anything else to have some intellectual tit for tat. He'd come to pay his respects to an unauthorized rabbi. The rabbi could surely pay his respects back by engaging in a discussion of abstract issues.

But Jesus was candid in a way this man had not expected. He was turning mind to mind into heart to heart. He was probing his innermost impulses and prejudices. Nicodemus was prepared for the truth. He wasn't prepared for the touch.

People who encountered Jesus often had that experience. His rivals constantly wanted to debate. They tried to trap him, catch him saying something that could be interpreted as unorthodox. It was a three-year running battle.

They kept scheming. Jesus kept touching.

A woman caught cheating on her husband is dragged before Jesus in the temple courtyard. The Pharisees want to corner him with the truth of Moses' law: shouldn't we stone this adulteress? Jesus scribbles a few things in the dirt with his finger. Perhaps he records a few of their own secret sins, because when he invites any sinless person present to throw the first stone, they slink away. And then he quietly covers the woman's humiliation with grace. There's no one left to condemn.

One day a scribe tries to draw him into their endless controversy about *who exactly is my neighbor?* Where could one truthfully draw the line? Jesus showed them the touch of the good Samaritan; he showed them how someone they despised could be a good neighbor to a stranger.

Some people are clamped down on the truth, and yet miles from the touch. Being right when everybody else is wrong has great appeal to certain individuals. Usually, it's because they weren't nurtured as children. They never learned how to receive love and give love in a healthy way. They can only be right in the sense of being correct—they've got the real facts, the inside information. So they argue a lot.

A truck driver once misjudged the height of an overpass and jammed his semi underneath it. The truck wouldn't budge. He was standing there on the side of the road, fuming at his predicament, when a motorist stopped and asked one of those really dumb questions: "Are you stuck?"

The driver replied acidly, "No, I was delivering this stupid bridge and I lost the address." Well, the insecure individual really *does* want people to believe he's delivering the bridge. He's not stuck, period.

Our first instinct, when confronted with someone who has to be right is, of course, to prove how wrong she is. We try to argue her into being a more loving human being. We want to back her into a corner so she will be more balanced.

But this is a game she's been playing a long time and knows how to win, or at least appear to win. She's got all the psychological self-help talk down and can maneuver her way through it to best advantage. She's got proof texts piled up in her closet. Our attempts to prove the contrary only make her argue more passionately for her position. She instinctively feels that if she's not right, she's not anything. And so she will go to great lengths to keep from being argued right out of existence.

Jesus suggests a different strategy. It's true, sometimes he did debate the Pharisees. Sometimes he did expose their hypocrisy in order to loosen their oppressive hold on devout Jews. But his ministry was driven by something else: touching people's real needs, touching their hidden thirsts.

It's possible to hammer home the truth and cover all the bases and prove all the points and still not touch human longing. We can pry open people's guilt and show them what they need to do, clear as day, and yet remain a clanging bell or a clashing cymbal, a sound they listen to politely but remain unmoved by.

Telling the truth without having the touch is like describing notes of music instead of playing them. A critic once remarked, tongue in cheek, "Wagner's music is better than it sounds." Sometimes our truth is better than it sounds.

Think of the day four guys lowered a paralyzed man on a mat right in front of Christ as he delivers a sermon. The Master Physician takes one look at the man's face and knows exactly how he needs to be touched. It's guilt that's shutting him down. It's an immoral lifestyle that has led to this physical collapse. And he's in agony about it. It's screaming so loudly inside his head, he can't even speak.

So Jesus leans over and says, "Take heart, son; your sins are forgiven."

Pharisee observers in the room immediately take note. Here's an opportunity to prove Jesus wrong. Only God can forgive sins. What greater truth is there than that?

Jesus, however, makes his case as the Messiah, as God-in-the-flesh, with a touch. He asks the paralyzed man to get up. The withered limbs promptly comply. Walking through the crowded house and outside to where his friends are climbing down from the roof, the man becomes a living monument to the liberating power of forgiveness.

Jesus has a penetrating touch. That is part of his charisma. He can get through to the real need. Some people wonder why they can't make friends and influence people when they've got so much truth on their side. Well, they probably haven't got the touch. And that's the biggest symptom of having the truth!

It's our privilege to touch as Jesus did. Instead of just arguing about the merits of Living Water, we can touch people's hidden thirst.

> The truth says, "You're looking for love in all the wrong places." The touch shows, "You could fall for the right Messiah."
>
> The truth says, "Don't worship things instead of the Creator." The touch asks, "Are you looking for something more?"
>
> The truth says, "Your addictions can never fill the holes inside." The touch promises, "Love can fill you up."
>
> The truth says, "Indifference to God is fatal." The touch suggests, "God has been trying to reach you."

Something wonderful happens when a human being's deepest longings are touched. Each of us has the chance somewhere, sometime, to give a name to desires so intense people can hardly give them words, to aches so deep they've lost a handle. We can do it with a touch, a gesture, a word, an act that says we see; we can imagine what's there in the heart.

So look past the calloused laugh and the nervous hands.

Look past the frown that's about to become a permanent face-print. That voice jagged as a saw blade was touched by love once and is tormented by its absence. Those hard eyes that disdain purity are still haunted by the possibility.

The standard-issue human heart isn't made out of numbers in need of the proper sum. It's made out of groans and intimations. That's what binds us together as human beings on this troubled planet. We have an idea there's more to life than this.

Jesus' touch is about fanning that idea into flame. It's about giving it color and shape. It's about sharing a longing that echoes someone else's. We often touch best by being vulnerable ourselves, sharing some hurt, some question, some unfulfilled desire. We don't have to have all the answers neatly organized to reach out. It's something else that turns the light on in people's eyes. It's the honest struggle to know. It's a journey toward the source of fulfillment. It's a feeling that the deepest dreams can come true.

Touch people in that way, and you've struck gold.

Every time Besim Zecevic jumped through the window to avoid exploding grenades, that same phrase stuck in his mind, "Come unto me."* It was inscribed in front of the church where he and

---

*This story is recorded by Filip Besim Zecevic in *Cover Me!* (Hagerstown, Md.: Review & Herald, 2000).

four buddies had sought refuge. They were trying to defend their Muslim hometown of Derventa, Bosnia, from the Serbs, who kept pushing back the demarcation line day by day, shell by shell, sniper by sniper. The phrase made him angry. It seemed such a stupid, empty invitation. What had this Jesus done for anyone caught up in the horrors of this war?

At one point Besim pointed his machine gun at the inscription, gripped by an urge to blast it away. But he didn't pull the trigger. After all, there were craters in a circle all around the church, but no shell had found the five of them inside. It almost seemed God was looking out for his house.

But such thoughts didn't come often. Besim was trapped in a world fighting to be right. Serbs, Croats, and Bosnians argued passionately about who had endured the worst atrocities. Many Muslims, Catholics, and Orthodox had come to believe their faith could survive only if they exterminated enemies.

So many ideologies. So many causes. So much religion at war. How do you stay sane in this environment? Besim did it by making fun of everything. He and his buddies mocked the mortars sent their way, mocked the snipers trying to pick them off, mocked the crazy bits of luck that determined who lived and who died every day.

Life was a long, long way from making any sense. And so they tried not to value it. They tried to face death with nonchalance.

One night Besim decided to kill time by reading one of the

Bibles in the church. He actually had to wrench one free from a stack that had been bound together by bullets shot through them. Locating the book with the fewest holes, he made it through three chapters of Genesis. The stories were familiar, but they seemed annoyingly odd now. Why did God place the curse on Eve and the serpent? What was the point?

There just didn't seem any room for faith in Besim's world. No one his age could believe the things they'd learned in mosque as kids. Allah wasn't scoring many points with them in this slaughter. And Besim certainly couldn't believe in the Christian God of his enemies. He had too much to forget. Like the woman in the red sweater.

She had walked out into the street one day while Besim was on duty. Seconds before, he'd spotted a camouflaged Serb soldier scanning the street with his rifle raised. Besim lifted his own weapon to fire at the soldier—and hesitated. He'd never killed anyone he could actually see, just fired at enemy positions.

Then the woman in the red sweater appeared. The Serb stepped up to her and fired at point-blank range. She dropped silently to the ground. The soldier walked away without a hint of emotion.

Besim couldn't get the red sweater out of his mind. And that was just one of the many, many things he had to try to forget.

Eventually, the Muslim soldiers were forced out of Derventa. Besim fought in Bosanski Brod. Sometimes he had to camp so close to enemy lines that even a whisper would draw fire. At night, huddled in a trench, Besim would look up at the silent constellations. His world consisted of dirt and blood, hate and ugliness. The stars spoke of light and beauty. Random cruelty dominated down here. Order and predictability seemed to rule up there. There was just no understanding it all.

One morning he woke up to find the town deserted. Then the bombs began to fall. Besim got some friends in a car and darted through the explosions across a bridge into Croatia.

He decided to make his own separate peace with the war, away from the Serbs. There was no longer any Derventa to defend. Besim had heard his sister was living in the city of Marusevac. He walked and hitchhiked all the way there and found her living in an old castle that housed a small Protestant college. What was she doing with these Christians?

As it turned out, they were quite friendly folk and persuaded him to stay a few days until he got his bearings. One of the school lecturers even helped him obtain a release from military conscription.

Besim attended one of their worship services, out of politeness, and found he enjoyed it. People shared honestly about their lives and sang choruses to God with real feeling. Above all, no one was arguing with him; no one was trying to be right. He'd come from the other side. He'd come straight from the front lines, where Muslims and Christians were still settling ancient scores with grenades. These kids didn't seem to notice. They just wanted to help him get on with his life. A few days later, one of the young women at the church brought him a bagful of clothes, a complete wardrobe the young men had put together from their own closets. Besim praised Allah that he'd landed among such good people.

People like Ivan. Besim had never met any human being so joyful about his faith. He kept telling Besim how wonderful Jesus the Savior was. Besim had no idea what he was supposed to be saved from, but he couldn't help admire the man's spirit. And it was so pleasant talking with him; it seemed the perfect vacation from a long war. Ivan wasn't trying to argue Besim into another ideology. It wasn't about taking sides. It wasn't about getting certain doctrines right. It was about an experience that was lighting up Ivan's life.

Some nights Besim wandered from café to café in the city, hoping to hear news about Derventa from the many Bosnian refugees hanging around. What he saw was just one hollow face after another. In bluish light filtering through cigarette smoke, the stories seemed to follow one sad plot. Everyone discussed the misery of his life; no one had the guts to change anything.

Finally, Besim decided to start classes at the Protestant school. And there he learned just what lay behind Ivan's enthusiasm. It made a lot of sense. It made a lot of sense even in 1993 in the ruins of what had been Yugoslavia. The more Besim learned, the more he began to feel that those bright stars up there just might have the last word. He began to catch signs that God had been with him through the whole bloody ordeal.

Besim wasn't mocking anymore. His longings were out in the open now, undisguised, unrepressed. And one day he decided that invitation, "Come to me," wasn't so ridiculous after all.

After his commitment, he described exactly how Jesus touched the deepest part of him:

> I felt something happening inside. God was creating a
> new man within me. At first I hardly knew how to
> react. There seemed to be a stranger in my body.
> Everything around me acquired a new sense of reality.
> I felt the existence of each separate leaf. Each stone
> had its weight and shape. Each letter on the page
> brimmed with reality. Every object in my life had its
> own peculiar warmth, its own shape and size. I was
> like a baby, learning about the world all over again. Up
> until that time events of my life passed through my
> experience as if they were some kind of movie I
> watched from afar, something unreal. Suddenly I lived
> in the *now*, I experienced reality.

That's what happens when the touch backs up the truth. Our hidden longings turn to gold. It's the most profound kind of persuasion.

Cited:

Nicodemus' visit — John 3:1-21

Caught in adultery — John 8:1-11

Good Samaritan — Luke 10:25-37

Paralyzed man — Mark 2:1-12

Your sins are forgiven — Matthew 9:2

THE HABITS OF AN ENEMY

I T WAS a lovely Sabbath day. The blue of Lake Galilee shimmered in morning light, not far from the Capernaum synagogue where Jesus was explaining Scripture. He was just beginning to get through. The people suddenly realized this man had some inside scoop on the big plan. And that's when it happened. The hecklers. They were always popping up when you least expected them. Some guy in back began yelling to wake the dead: "What do you want with us, Jesus of Nazareth? Have you come to destroy us?"

Jesus didn't take kindly to the interruption. He didn't reason with the man. He didn't try to disarm him with a gentle touch. He gave a quick, stern command: "Be quiet! . . . Come out of him!"

Immediately the man gave a shriek and collapsed on the pavement, shaking violently. They had to carry him out.

Sometimes the Man with the Golden Touch could touch pretty hard. That tender hand of the good Shepherd was attached to a strong arm. When he flipped over the tables of the moneychangers and merchants in the temple courtyard—for the second time—officials couldn't believe they'd all fled the scene, again. No one could stand his ground before him.

When the most violent lunatics in Galilee came rushing up to Jesus, dragging broken chains and making beastly noises, they suddenly found themselves blubbering at his feet, pleading for mercy, just because he asked them their name.

Jesus could stop some heavy traffic with his outstretched hand. And that is part of the secret of his great charisma. It's one thing to express love and understanding to everyone because you're a wimp and you don't have other options. It's quite another to touch with grace when you could just as easily smash into the ground. The no-nonsense fishermen and farmers of Galilee were awed by this man because they sensed the boundless power behind his gentle touch.

Sometimes a firm hand is required to find hidden treasure. It's true that Christ's touch compels us to look for the good, not the bad. We take on hopeless cases and affirm bits of faith and appreciate the smallest gifts. But in some cases we have to draw a clear line before we can dig for nuggets. We have to do this because some people are enemies not because we see them that way; they're enemies because they're trying to hurt us.

Jesus had to deal with real enemies. The man yelling in the synagogue wasn't just having a bad day on the farm. He was being used by a force bent on destroying the Messiah. He was part of a conspiracy to subvert Jesus' ministry.

Jesus had to deal with religious rivals, people who spent

their days trying to figure out how to trip him up, how to make him look bad, how to get the upper hand.

Some people need to be resisted. Some people are trying to hurt us, or control us, or manipulate us. And they will keep doing this as long as we let them.

It won't do to look for hidden treasure there with a limp wrist or passive hand. We'll never find it. Dysfunctional behavior continues until it hits a brick wall. It doesn't spontaneously get better. Letting mean people walk over you won't get them somewhere else. They'll stay in their rut.

So how do we protect ourselves from enemies without throwing away grace? Is that possible? Do we just have to look for hidden treasure somewhere else?

Jesus shows us just the right touch at the end of his Last Supper. He'd washed everyone's feet. He'd cleared the air. And now, with this last meal before his execution, he wanted to bond the Twelve to himself. This was the church that had to overcome the world. Jesus looked around at the men munching on bread and fish, and knew he had to bond them around something they didn't want to think about: his broken body and shed blood. But there was something he had to do first. He had to draw a line.

Looking quite pained, Jesus said, "One of you is going to betray me."

Shocked silence. Then worried glances. Then a few indignant questions: Surely not I, Lord?

Finally, Peter nudged John and whispered, "Ask him which one he means."

John did. And Jesus broke the tense silence. "It is the one to whom I will give this piece of bread."

Slowly and deliberately, just as he had when he took these men's soiled feet in his hands, Jesus dipped a piece of bread into a bowl of herbs and stretched it out to Judas Iscariot. The disciples gasped. They looked at each other. No one wanted to believe this. How could their chief financial officer be the enemy?

But Jesus held it out, hand steady as a rock. This was a gesture that typically honored a guest. And in fact, Jesus was offering his broken body to the man on the verge of betrayal. He was extending the emblems of a great sacrifice. But he was doing it in a way that forced Judas' hand. He would have to make a decision. That bit of dripping bread told him, "To stay here you are going to have to acknowledge your betrayal."

Their eyes met. Judas took the morsel, but then he blinked. He opened his mouth to speak, but the confession didn't come. He wouldn't admit face to face what he'd been doing behind Jesus' back.

And so the Master drew the line. "What you are about to do, do quickly." Judas couldn't stay. He gathered his cloak about him and walked out into the night.

Christ had no problem socializing with people who had all kinds of moral problems. He didn't need to stay away in order to show disapproval. But here was someone bent on hurting him. Judas may have imagined, in his tangled mind, he could force Jesus to declare himself king, to become the kind of messiah he thought Jesus should be. But Judas was playing into the hands of Christ's enemies. And so Jesus put up a stop sign: *Don't come any closer. You can't betray me and still pretend to be my disciple.*

What's so revealing about Jesus' firm hand in this scene is the way he drew that boundary. He was still, in fact, looking for hidden treasure. He still wanted this tormented man to be his disciple. *Here's the bread. I'm offering it to you. But you're going to have to square things up in order to truly receive it.*

Jesus shows us how to draw boundaries and still retain a hidden-treasure perspective. First of all, he teaches us *when* to draw the line. We draw the line when people are hurting us, or hurting those we're responsible for. We don't draw the line when people are hurting themselves.

If people do things to themselves that annoy you, or that you disapprove of, that's the wrong time to draw a line, the wrong time to exclude. Saying, "I won't be your friend unless you stop eating all that junk food," is controlling. It's the wrong touch. Drawing a line to say, "You're not living up to my standards," is the wrong touch. Counseling with them as a friend is the right touch.

However, saying, "I can't let you in my house if you keep abusing me and the kids," is a good boundary. You're not writing anyone off as a hopeless case. You're making sure you don't provide aid and comfort to dysfunctional behavior.

We can't make people change by drawing lines. But we can stop people from hurting us. You can't always judge if someone is hurting herself. But you can judge what's hurting you.

Jesus hung out with tax collectors and prostitutes. They were messed up. But he could help them as a friend. Jesus stood up to the Pharisees who were trying to harm him and his disciples. He had to draw that line if he was ever going to get through their self-righteous barriers to hidden treasure.

Paul made a pledge to Corinthian believers who were struggling with everything from incest to lawsuits in the church: "You are in our hearts to die together and to live together." He could plead with them as a friend. Paul stood up to divisive people who were tearing up congregations with their slander. They had to be isolated; they were harming those he was responsible for.

The second thing Jesus' touch at the Last Supper teaches is *how* to draw the line. We resist destructive people best by using our strengths, not their weaknesses. The soft touch needs a strong arm, a show of strength. Part of that is a refusal to fight back with their weapons.

Jesus didn't plot behind Judas's back in order to counteract Judas's plots behind his back. He didn't try to secretly undermine Judas's position with the moneybags. Jesus resisted Judas by showing who he was. *This is me, this broken body. I'm all about the loving thing to do, period. I'm not going to manipulate you into the loving thing to do. But I'm going to prevent you from breaking apart the love in this circle of disciples.* Difficult people always want us to fight back with their weapons.

They want us to get fixed on their negative input, their put-downs, sleights, insinuations. And they want us to fight back in kind—because they can always win that kind of altercation. You can't out-negative them:

A driven, bossy, difficult person wants to lock horns with you: Let's see who can push the hardest. He may try to shame you into his mold: You're a softy, an airhead. If you try to fight back in his way, you'll lose. If you mirror his negative traits, you'll come up short.

An introverted difficult person wants to manipulate by drawing you into her web of resentment and perfectionist criticism. She analyzes things to death. You can't out-dissect her. She wins all the intellectual games.

An impulsive, out-of-control person may try to draw you into his chaotic life, perhaps make you responsible for bailing him out. Well, you can't overwhelm him with your stuff. You can't out-talk him. You can't interrupt him more than he interrupts you. You'll always lose.

Jesus' touch inspires us to say "no" with our positive traits, our strengths. Lead with who you are. If you know who you are, difficult people won't try to change you into who they are.

You can walk away from the yeller if you can hear your
own quiet voice.

You can refuse the back-stabber's alliance if you are
confident in your own friendships.

You can avoid taking responsibility for the melancholic's
mood if you know your own breezy cheer is just as
authentic.

You can step away from the anger if you see yourself as
a peacemaker.

You can decline the narrow, mean-spirited point of view
if you believe in the bigger picture.

In a study of songbirds, those raised in isolation did not
learn the characteristic chirp of their species. They could even
be trained to imitate the songs of other birds. But as soon as
they heard their natural song, they learned it quickly and sang
only that.

Know your song. Don't march to the beat of another drum-
mer just because it's playing loudly in your ear.

Drawing a line helps us create our own authentic space.
That in itself is a treasure. But drawing a line can also uncover
something good in difficult people. Sometimes it persuades
them to deal with their stuff. Sometimes Judas doesn't walk out
the door. There's no greater gold than turning an enemy into a
friend who respects who you are.

———— 〰 ————

The stairs leading up to the master bedroom seemed very long that night. There were plenty of things pulling Nathan away from the first step. I remember him telling me about them.

There were little pieces of cooked corn and carrot slowly sliding down the glass door to the patio. That's where Cynthia had thrown a vegetable dish in her profound frustration.

Nathan always feared what she might do if he really confronted her. Cynthia didn't take any hint of criticism well. Once, during an argument, she'd threatened to drive off in their car and get in an accident.

There were her sobs in the middle of the night as she slept downstairs in the den. She was terribly lonely, but wanted to be alone. He would go down and hold her and try to speak comforting words, but her misery was always deeper than anything he could reach.

There was her abrupt and absolute cutting off of their dearest friends. She got depressed whenever he tried to contact them, accused him of not being supportive. How could he, and have a normal life? The pain of a childhood without nurture was now driving her to places he could not follow.

Above all, there was his long habit of saying, "I'm sorry; I'll try to do better." Wasn't that what a good husband did? He was supposed to fix things—fix his wife's unhappiness, fix her moods. Yes, she seemed to blame all her problems on his failure to listen enough, to understand enough. But there was always room for improvement. He could always do better.

All these things made Nathan's feet feel like lead as he contemplated the carpeted stairway. The thought of how Cynthia might fall apart even further, the thought of what seeing that might do to their kids, paralyzed him.

And yet he moved. He willed his legs to trudge up the stairs for only one reason. The anger and resentment he'd been stuffing down for years was just too great. It was making him physically ill. It was making him realize something was terribly wrong.

Nathan walked into the bedroom where Cynthia was reading yet another self-help book and said, "I've come to realize I'm really, really angry." Cynthia sat up in the king-sized bed, flashing fear in her eyes.

Nathan walked to the window, looked out at the giant bird of paradise trees in the back yard, and spilled his emotions. He felt criticized all the time and he kept trying but it was never enough. He felt dumped on a lot.

Cynthia jumped to her own rescue. Hadn't he noticed how much she'd been growing lately? The real issue was that she was having a wonderful new experience with God and he was lagging far behind, stuck in his comfort zone.

Nathan sat on the foot of the bed. "So why are you so miserable?"

Now Cynthia really erupted. She threw the list at him, the list of all the things he was doing to keep her isolated in her pain. And Nathan found himself slowly shaking his head as she ran through the accusations. "No, that's it. I'm not going to take the rap anymore." He said it quietly and surely underneath her wailing.

Cynthia redoubled her efforts. He just never tried to understand her point of view. He was always caught up in his own little world. Nathan stood up and found steel in his voice: "Not agreeing with you is not the same as not understanding! I'm sick to death of this whole mess, the manipulation. You will never, never do this to me again!"

Nathan meant it. And to his great surprise, Cynthia actually began changing. A few nights later she was apologizing for her behavior as a wife. She accepted the fact that what she really needed to do was to love Nathan. "You deserve much better."

Nathan embraced her, murmuring, "I need you desperately," and she melted in his arms. It wasn't just a one-night stand on principle. In the weeks and months that followed, Cynthia did stop blaming; she tried to be helpful.

Nathan was blown away. All his life he'd avoided conflict as a way to keep peace with those he loved. And now he'd risked everything by drawing a firm boundary and, what do you know, found hidden treasure in his wife. He was actually sleeping at night now, getting much healthier. Their lovemaking became more passionate than ever. There was still a lot of work for them to do, and they began counseling to deal with issues that had driven them to play their roles for so long. But there was hope. There was an opportunity to uncover gold where before there had been only pain and accusation.

Cited:

The heckler—Mark 1:21-28

Second cleansing of the temple—Mark 11:15-18

Violent lunatics—Mark 5:1-20

Last Supper, Judas—John 13:21-30

You are in our hearts—2 Corinthians 7:3 (NASB)

THE SORROW OF GUILT

H E WAS hanging there like a frozen crime. The violence of an assault visible in his distended limbs. The violation of a rape painfully clear in the spikes driven into his wrists and ankles. The cruelty of a murder evident in the blood pouring down his face from a crown of thorns.

Jesus had been made a spectacle on a hill just outside Jerusalem in order to inspire lawfulness. The Romans designed crucifixions to stop short those who might be thinking about larceny or insurrection.

But darker forces were at work as well above the soldiers gambling for his discarded cloak. These forces had a different point to make. Soldiers mocking him, priests taunting him, followers fleeing the scene—they all followed a script written centuries before. This was theater for the ages. God had one climax in mind, but his enemies quite another. Human animosity and jealousy, along with its counterpart in the heavens, desperately worked to make this execution come out a certain way. Jesus had to be kept from saying one thing at all costs. He had to be kept from saying, "I forgive you," when the curtain came down.

That's where the plot was headed. You could see it foreshadowed in Christ's words as he was nailed to the beams. Lying there with the first jagged agony ripping through his body, Jesus looked up at the clouds gathering overhead and made a request. He wanted the Father to forgive the soldiers with the hammer. They were just playing their bit parts in the drama, after all, unaware that this was the blood of God's Son spurting out on the ground.

Jesus was hell-bent on forgiving. So, hate had to work feverishly. Surely if this man were tortured enough, his own cries of pain would drown out the pardon. Surely if priests tried to provoke him into deserting the cross he would do so—and not forgive. If the keepers of the covenant that pointed to him didn't get it, who would? And above all, if the Father himself abandoned him to his fate, surely he would not extend divine forgiveness. How could he? He wasn't getting any in the hour of greatest need.

Lightning flashed. Thunder rumbled. The earth shook. The drama was building toward its climax. And then the tension reached a breaking point. Two thieves crucified on either side of Jesus joined in the mocking. At least that's what it looked like as the more vocal one called out, "Aren't you the Christ? Save yourself and us!" He was hurling the same insults as the soldiers and priests who urged the great miracle worker to do one more for the show.

That should have been the last straw. Dying thieves, men on the verge of heaven or hell—poking a little fun? Having a cruel joke at the expense of their eternal destiny? That's too much. Christ's companions in crime represented all of imperfect humanity, convicted of wrongdoing, standing in great need of pardon. And they were just spitting it away! Why in the world go through this ordeal? Why experience hell for people who pretend the judgment doesn't exist?

That was the moment when the plot could have twisted disastrously. Everything could have been lost. Jesus could have given the mockers exactly what they asked for. Talk about poetic justice!

But Jesus wouldn't budge. It was his greatest act of courage. He kept silent, waiting to deliver the last redemptive lines at the last moment. He wouldn't bow out beforehand.

And that's when a light broke through the clouds. One of the thieves thought better of the insults snarling around the central cross. He decided to shut up at least one scoffer. Gathering up his breath, he reminded the other thief they'd been condemned as lawbreakers. Maybe a little fear of God was in order. And then he glanced at the face of the one who claimed to be Messiah and said, "We are punished justly. . . . But this man has done nothing wrong."

The thief must have seen some ground for hope in the eyes of Jesus looking back at him, because he said, "Remember me when you come into your kingdom."

That was all Jesus needed. It was done. God would have his

happy ending to the tragedy. Christ delivered the solemn assurance, "You will be with me in paradise."

Hell happened and forgiveness happened. That's the story. Jesus breathed his last and the curtain in the temple was torn from top to bottom, indicating that the drama of ages had finished. It had played out according to grace.

One of the most amazing things about Jesus' reach is that he continued touching even when his limbs were bound tightly to a cross. He kept looking for hidden treasure until his very last breath. And what Jesus touched so dramatically on Golgotha was human guilt. He touched that universal human ailment in a certain way, and sin would never be the same. Because of that final touch, forgiveness shot up in the scale of things. It leaped from nice gesture to transforming force.

On the cross, Jesus made guilt touchable. He stretched out his arms and now guilt is no longer something inaccessible, like a repressed memory. It's not something we have to tiptoe around, like an incurable disease. It's not something so toxic it forces us to put up barriers against contamination.

When Jesus forgave the thief hanging beside him, he disarmed guilt in a very profound way. This was a last-minute pardon. The condemned man couldn't make up for his crimes. He couldn't serve time for them. He wouldn't be doing many good deeds in the few moments between forgiveness and death.

Jesus' promise to his dying companion makes it quite clear

that guilt isn't removed by elbow grease, like a stain on your carpet. It's removed by a touch, a word. That's it.

Guilt holds people hostage. It haunts us with the impossibility of making up for what we've done. We may try to atone, but there's always more to atone for. Jesus' touch changes all that. It unleashes a wholly undeserved grace in the human drama. Jesus earned the right to forgive. He made guilt touchable.

That's the good news. But it gets even better. And it gets harder. Jesus' touch also shows us that we can find hidden treasure in guilt. We can find it in the person who has wronged us, who needs to make up for something she's done to us.

Our natural response, of course, is to strike back. Yes, we do indeed want a payback for the pain that person brought us. We want the one who caused suffering to suffer. Wrongs done to us are something we chew on for years.

Abraham Lincoln, the president who worked so hard at reconciliation, liked to tell the story of the Illinois farmer laid up with a fatal illness. His family suggested that, seeing how he was facing eternity, he might want to put things right with a neighbor whom he blamed for a cattle deal gone bad. The farmer agreed to send a message of let-bygones-be-bygones. As they were about to walk out with the letter, however, he rose up on his pillow and called out, "But if I recover, tell him the feud is still on."

Forgiveness isn't something we dispense easily. It's like being asked to make a contribution when we're a bit short on cash.

Our instinct is to dole it out in pennies. We want to make sure none of it is wasted on the undeserving.

But this kind of thriftiness ends up siphoning off our own emotional reserves. We lose heart. The hurt still takes up space in there. It's a debt we haven't quite erased, and the frustrated longing for payment will eventually wear us down.

Jesus' touch at the cross inspires something else. Christ's pardon isn't rationed, as if there were only so much to go around. He didn't hand out just enough to get the dying thief out of his last jam. He sent him all the way to paradise. Forgiveness spilled out of him as dramatically as the blood gushing from his wounds. Well, if God can be that generous to us, we can afford to waste a little ourselves.

A good look at the cross can loosen us up. We can deliver a full pardon when someone comes with his sorrow and repentance. We can pour out the whole thing. Give it up. Don't just dab a little water of absolution on the forehead; try total immersion.

It's in lavishing forgiveness that we find hidden treasure. That's the touch. Stingy, grudging acknowledgments of an apology won't get us to any gold. Forgiveness needs to be the last word. All debts cancelled. No reserved clauses in the contract. Nothing left over to be settled later.

As we've seen, sometimes an effectively soft touch requires a strong arm. Sometimes we have to draw boundaries to protect ourselves. But something different is called for when we are confronted with the sorrow of the guilty. That's a huge opportunity. We can turn that sorrow into a meaningful transaction by the touch of forgiveness. It can happen either by offering forgiveness ourselves, when called for, or by pointing the person to the forgiveness God offers.

In the shadow of these arms extended on the cross,

> Grace starts to weigh more than the grudge.
> Getting over it rings truer than getting even.
> Meeting face to face calls louder than stabbing in the
> back.
> A prayer for genuine sorrow comes quicker than a
> prayer for sweet revenge.

What Jesus expressed in his hour of betrayal and abandonment can impel us to open our arms when human nature wants to make a fist. We can touch guilt as Jesus did. It's our choice. In Christ's economy, forgiveness isn't just an obligation. It's more than just absolving the little debts others owe us so that God will cancel our big one. It's more than just therapy, a way to get over the hurt. In Christ's economy, forgiveness is the way to find hidden treasure. He suggests that the greatest rewards often come to those who have the most to forgive.

Driving north on Highway 101 out of the L.A. basin, Susan could still see obscenities scrawled on the living room wall in her mother's blood.* It had been eighteen years, but the brutal crime had not lost its power to shock and outrage. And now she was finally going to confront the perpetrator.

Passing apartment complexes in the San Fernando Valley, Susan could taste the nauseating horror that overwhelmed her the night she walked into her parents' home and found their knifed bodies, victims of Charles Manson's "Helter Skelter."

Meantime, an unsuspecting inmate of the Men's Colony in San Luis Obispo waited for a visitor. The visits of Charles Watson, "Manson's Executioner," were strictly regulated. They had to be scheduled months in advance. A woman who'd been corresponding with him for some time was coming to see him. She'd responded sympathetically to his descriptions of the faith he'd found in prison. She'd asked a lot of questions about his Christianity. She'd gained his trust.

But she hadn't mentioned Rosemary LaBianca, her mother. She hadn't mentioned the fear that shadowed her for years after the murders. She hadn't described driving around all night until the sun came up because she was too scared to go home.

---

*This story is recorded in the following sources: Jessica Shaver, "Daughter of Manson Victims Finds Forgiveness," *Christianity Today,* Sept. 22, 1989, pp. 50-51; Brian Bird, "Twenty Years After Helter Skelter," *Moody,* July/August 1989, pp. 24-27; and "The Miracle of Forgiveness," "The Cost of Forgiveness," Charles and Kristin Watson, Abounding Love Ministries, Jackson, Calif., 1992.

Now Susan was driving with her hands firmly on the wheel, rehearsing what she might say to this man. Passing the beaches of Santa Barbara, she couldn't help recalling the lost years when she buried her anger in drugs and parties, unable to talk to anyone about her loss.

Below the guard towers, Charles Watson paced the prison yard, wondering what Susan might be like, what she would think of him face to face. Everyone knew about the Tate-LaBianca bloodbath, of course. Everyone knew about the hippie kids seeking to live wild and free on acid who fell under Manson's spell. It was painfully obvious Watson and three girls had obeyed his orders to "make it as gruesome as possible."

Susan knew about that. But she didn't know everything. She couldn't know about the horrifying vacuum inside this former University of Texas frat boy. He looked back and knew he was barely human. The day after the eight homicides, the only thing Watson felt was fatigue. No guilt. No shame. Just sore muscles. It had taken him years to grasp the evil of what had happened that night.

Arriving at the prison, Susan walked up to the visitor's gate and a long line of people. It would be a two-hour wait, she was told. Susan stayed. She'd already been waiting almost two decades. Finally, she got through the gates and searches and had her wrist stamped with an ultraviolet code.

Walking toward the visiting room, she knew the moment

had come. She could tell this man, who could never make up for his crimes, just what he'd done to her. She could unload what was on her heart—in a way she hadn't been able to with her parents. They'd died so suddenly. Susan had never been able to say she was sorry for all she put them through as a rebellious teenager. That missing apology had ached for a long time. This man had taken it from her.

Susan LaBerge and Charles Watson sat facing each other and exchanged a few pleasantries. They began talking about their respective histories. At length, Watson realized both of them had been in L.A. at the time of his crimes.

So Susan dropped the bomb: "Rosemary LaBianca was my mother."

Watson didn't want to believe her at first. Maybe this was a hoax. Maybe this woman was a nut. But slowly, point by point, Susan began revealing things about her family no one else could know.

As Watson sat there stunned, she delivered the blow. But it wasn't at all what he might have expected. She had come all the way from New Mexico, not in search of revenge, but in search of hidden treasure. Something had happened to her after those lost years. She had discovered the touch of Christ's forgiveness and he had begun to put her life back together again. And now she made a decision. Looking at this man with the clear, sensitive eyes, she could accept the stories people in prison told of his transformation. She could accept the fact that years of coming to terms with his crimes had produced genuine repentance. This was a brother in the faith. Susan was ready to forgive.

The blood on the wall, the mangled bodies, the animal cruelty—all that stood between these two human beings in the visitor's room. It was more vivid than it had been in years. But instead of accusation and rage, something else was exchanged that day. Susan and Charles sat for a long time, often too overwhelmed to speak, tears streaming down their faces.

Susan had touched his guilt. Charles would come to "see myself through the eyes of the people whose lives I damaged." He would identify with the victims even more. But he could also seek forgiveness face to face.

And Susan soared: "I felt so light, so free, and so unburdened. It took the boogeyman out of the murders and brought many things into perspective."

Toward the end of their encounter, the two clutched hands and prayed, aware that a miracle had just passed between them. To Watson it seemed like he was being baptized by this "physical act of forgiveness."

Susan continued corresponding with Charles after the visit, sharing much more now. And she found herself maturing spiritually, growing in new ways through the letters. She and Charles came to believe that "healing took place that could have never happened any other way."

In extending Christ's forgiving touch, Susan did indeed find hidden treasure. She found the love of a Christian brother where before there had been only pain and regret. She found a bond that has brought two families together.

Forgiveness is Jesus' last word on the cross. It's the touch he leaves us with. This man was violated in ways we can't imagine. His body and mind and spirit were terribly transgressed. But he dealt with the wounds by creating a medicine for countless others. He dealt with it by looking forward to human beings coming to that cross with their sorrow. The cross is his way of making an irrevocable stand. No matter what, he will continue looking for hidden treasure.

He is mocked and stabbed, to be sure. But there's a sparkle of silver there in his glance at the tormenters. Suffocating, lifted up on spiked ankles, he catches a glimpse of a face just turning to tenderness. He's the spy, always on the lookout for random acts of repentance among the ragged and the hardened. Thunder crashes down; lightning blinds him. But his mind retains an image of a soldier's involuntary confession of faith.

He's surrounded by jealousy so malignant it requires an entire religion to hide it. But he's got an eye for the stray chick who might find shelter under his wings. Demonic forces have made a spectacle of humanity at its very worst. But that cross impaling the earth is really digging for buried fortunes. Like a 49er in the frenzy of a gold rush, he's a passionate miner, always going deeper than our wrongs, always grabbing for the gem in the rough.

His whole life is pouring out in blood that won't clot. The earth shakes. Crosses sway. But he stays upright. He's been uncovering treasure in sleepy goat towns and dusty fishing villages for three years and he's not leaving until it's done.

You can nail his arms to a cross. But he's still got the touch.

Cited:

Scene at the cross—Mark 15:1-41
Crucified thief—Luke 23:39-43

THE KEY TO THE GOLDEN TOUCH

H AVE YOU ever wondered why Jesus formed his chosen Twelve with men who were so radically different from each other? It was quite a collection.

Opposite temperaments: impulsive Peter who couldn't get his foot out of his mouth, versus calculating, controlled Judas who couldn't stop plotting behind the scenes.

Opposite ideologies: Simon the revolutionary Zealot, who'd worked to overthrow the Romans, versus Levi Matthew, who collected taxes for them.

Opposite mindsets: introverted skeptics like Thomas and Nathaniel, versus passionate advocates like John and James, the "sons of thunder."

I think Jesus was doing more with this group than just showing us a nice cross-section of humanity. He wanted this inner circle to model a very important principle: learning from opposites. Acquiring the touch that uncovers hidden treasure is largely based on that. In order to actually become disciples, the Twelve had to learn to stretch, instead of just react.

Several years ago I researched a variety of temperament and

personality tests in preparation for an international radio broad-
cast, a series called *How to Get Along with Just About Everybody*.
In the process we created a detailed picture of temperaments as a
spectrum of personality traits. People don't just occupy a certain
block of temperament. They practice a certain range of behavior
that lies somewhere on the scale between cheery and analytical,
between flexible and forceful, between impulsive and controlled.

And what we find is this: People who have a narrow range
of behavior have more conflicts. Individuals who are always
impulsive and never controlled are constantly butting heads
with people who are always controlled and never impulsive, for
example. As we saw in chapter 4, in a relationship these two
tend to push each other to extremes, trying to "make up for" the
failings of the other.

But the fact is, we can actually learn the most from those
who irritate us the most. What they have too much of, we need
more of. The impulsive person needs self-discipline more than
anything else—and the disciplined person needs to be more
impulsive. Instead of just reacting, instead of just retreating into
our trait, we need to stretch; we need to try out a wider range of
responses to life situations.

The same holds true for differences in ideology, differences
in economic status, differences in family of origin. The one we
instinctively turn off is often the one who has the most to give
us. And we may have a lot to give him. Stretching instead of

reacting can transform so many relationships.

The apostle Paul gave the Corinthians a wonderful reason to do just that. He emphasized the fact that "the light of the knowledge of the glory of God" shines in our hearts. "But we have this treasure in jars of clay." Most of the time we simply lament the fact that we're all jars of clay—and often trip up over those annoying imperfections in people around us. But the greater truth is that there is *treasure* in those "earthen vessels." That glow of Christ's light inside those jars of clay could be just the thing that illuminates your blind spot.

We need Jesus' touch today. It can get us past so much of the pettiness and animosity that can clog up our lives. It can cut through the emotional baggage that predisposes us to have problems with people. We've got the truth about how to be healthier. But we need the touch. We need that liberating habit of looking for hidden treasure.

There is gold in every person around us! That's the perspective that can make all the difference. It's the key to Christ's charismatic touch. And he not only shows us *how* to touch, he also shows us *what* to touch. The things he turned to gold spotlight exactly what we can stretch toward.

> When you're sinking into a comfortable rut, stretch
>   toward the noise of innocence.
> When you find your boundaries have become brick

walls, stretch toward the stare of a stranger.

When you're complaining about life's annoyances,
stretch toward the smallest of gifts.

When your faith starts to feel old, stretch toward
someone's first flicker.

When you've got everything under control, stretch
toward the messiness of affection.

When you start getting self-righteous, stretch toward a
hopeless case.

When you have to invest a lot of energy protecting a
secret, stretch toward the dirty truth.

When you've failed to get through with the truth, touch
someone's hidden thirst.

When you are threatened or manipulated, stretch out
with your strengths.

When you find yourself wronged, stretch out toward
sorrow with forgiveness.

In 1988 I was working in Rome on a television series called
Empires in Collision. While wandering through long, fresco-
filled corridors in the Vatican, I came upon the Sistine Chapel.
There in the middle stood a platform, rising on steel bars all the
way to the famous arched ceiling. A team of scientists and art
historians was busy restoring Michelangelo's masterpiece.
Craning my neck to look up, I saw a remarkable display of

before and after. On one side of the platform heroic biblical figures posed in bright garments and vivid flesh tones. On the other side, the colors lay muted under browns and grays.

As I would discover later, Renaissance experts had a hard time adjusting to the new and improved Michelangelo. Some even protested that the restoration process had distorted the painter's handiwork. These brilliant reds and greens on the prophets up there seemed cartoonish. The experts had come to believe their beloved Michelangelo had a much more somber take on life.

But of course what they'd been looking at was the grime of centuries. In the Middle Ages the chapel was often lit with torches and the soot from those flames had slowly, imperceptibly dulled the artist's biblical panorama.

But now, finally, people like me could see something much closer to the original. The figures jump out at you. There he was, the Almighty with Eve in the crook of his arm, stretching out his hand toward Adam, who stretched back. There it was, painted bold and larger than life, the touch that created the first living soul.

My before-and-after look at the Sistine Chapel has given me a memorable picture of what Jesus' touch is all about. Human beings have been accumulating a lot of grime over the centuries on this planet. God's original vision as Creator has been dulled and distorted. And many of us have come to believe the browns and grays are all there is. Human selfishness and cruelty and indifference—that's just the way we evolved; those are our truest instincts. Bright pictures of our fate are simply naïve.

But then Jesus comes along and carries off incredible feats of restoration. Suddenly, the bleak life sentence of a quadriplegic somersaults into ruddy health. Suddenly, the grimy gray lifestyle of a prostitute flips into pure devotion, fresh as a violet.

Jesus as the Redeemer who took on humanity can get people back to the original colors found in the Garden of Eden. And his love compels us to look at individuals in that light. As he said in his Sermon on the Mount: "You're here to be salt-seasoning that brings out the God-flavors of this earth. . . . You're here to be light, bringing out the God-colors in the world." We can indeed catch a hint of bright amber or magenta or blue underneath the dirty brown. And we are moved to reach out with his touch.

It's these simple acts of looking for hidden treasure that can profoundly change life on this planet. We can create a different panorama. We can extend the magic of the Man with the Golden Touch.

Cited:

The light of glory of God—2 Corinthians 4:6-7 (NASB, NIV)
Salt and light—Matthew 5:13-14 (MSG)

AUTHOR

STEVEN MOSLEY has been making the Bible come alive for contemporary audiences all over the world since 1984 as a scriptwriter and producer who has won Telly and Angel awards in Christian television. His telecast series include *Soul Care, Jesus Face to Face,* and *Truths That Change Us Inside.* He also conducts "Wield the Word" weekend seminars around the United States, featuring a dramatic presentation: "Chosen Garment—the Whole Bible in One Act."

Steven is the author of twelve books, including *Secrets of the Mustard Seed, Glimpses of God,* and *Great Stories and How to Tell Them.* He lives in Huntington Beach, California, with his wife, Marilyn. They are the parents of Jason, Jennifer, Austin, Parker, and Garrett.